Y0-BVQ-373

SERIAL No. B 1043

BOOK

BREACH OF SECURITY

BOOKS BY DAVID IRVING
The Destruction of Dresden
The Mare's Nest
The Virus House

BOOKS BY D. C. WATT
Britain Looks to Germany:
A Study of British Opinion and Policy towards Germany since 1945
Personalities and Policies:
Studies in the Formulation of British Foreign Policy in the 20th Century

With Frank Spencer and Neville Brown
A History of the World in the 20th Century

With K. Bourne
Studies in International History:
Essays presented to W. N. Medlicott

BREACH OF SECURITY

The German
Secret Intelligence File
on Events leading to the
Second World War

Edited by David Irving

with an Introduction by D. C. Watt,
Reader in International History in the
University of London

WILLIAM KIMBER
6 QUEEN ANNE'S GATE
LONDON SWI

First published in 1968 by
William Kimber and Co. Limited
6 Queen Anne's Gate, London S.W.1

© Introduction D. C. Watt, 1968

Translation and Editorial Matter
© William Kimber and Co. Limited 1968

Standard Book Number
SBN 7183 0101 3

327.42

Printed in Great Britain
by W & J Mackay & Co Ltd, Chatham

'A great part of the information obtained in war is contradictory, a still greater part is false and by far the greatest part is of a doubtful character.'

Clausewitz: *On War*

Contents

List of Illustrations

Preface

David Irving and Donald Watt wish to record their indebtedness to the several people who gave assistance in the preparation of this publication, and in particular to Mr C. J. Child, Librarian of the Foreign Office, and Dr Sasse of the political archives of the German Foreign Office in Bonn, for their invaluable help and assistance and for permission for the reproduction of the first document published here. We are also indebted to Dr Robert Wolfe of the National Archives, Washington, for drawing our attention to the document extracted in the first appendix. Our thanks are due to the Institut für Zeitgeschichte in Munich on two counts: Dr Anton Hoch provided the unpublished volumes of the Goebbels Diaries of which use has been made in the third appendix, and Dr Martin Broszat made available a penetrating study on the history of the Forschungsamt. Acknowledgement is also made to Mr L. Jackets of the Ministry of Defence, Historical Section, to Mr Brian Melland of the Cabinet Office, Historical Section and to Miss Angela Raspin of the Foreign Documents Centre of the Imperial War Museum.

In the document 'On British Policy from Munich to the Outbreak of War', and in the notes and related documents printed as appendices, we have followed the practice of putting the explanatory introductions and similar comments inside square brackets. Any opinions expressed in the Introduction and the editorial material are those of Donald Watt and David Irving respectively, and are not necessarily shared by the other.

Für heute können wir diese ..... (FA: nicht lesbar) folgendermassen zusammenfassen:

1) Man darf niemanden im Zweifel darüber lassen, dass wir gemäss dem Verlauf der Ereignisse, ...(FA: nicht lesbar). zu Gunsten der allge-meinen Friedensinteressen mit England gehen, oder eine (FA: nicht lesbar) Politik verfolgen, und dass wir neutral bleiben werden, solange die Achsenstaaten im Mittelmeer und auf dem Balkan nicht zum Angriff übergehen.

2) D.. grosse ..... (FA:nicht lesbar) muss schon jetzt unsere unternommen Abwehrvorbereitungen, uns nötigenfalls auf dem Lande gegen die Achsen-staaten zu wehren, unterstützen.

3) Man muss sich bemühen, um die Zusammenarbeit Sowjetrusslands sicherzustellen.

4) England muss seine Unterstützung dazu ge-währen, zwischen den Bulgaren und Rumänen einen Schritt zu .... (FA: nicht lesbar).

5) Daraufhin, dass wir im Einigungsfalle mit-marschieren, muss man uns schon heute über das in Ihrer Note besprochene Projekt Mitteilung machen.

6) Die oben aufgeführten Punkte und .....(FA:nicht lesbar) müssen vollkommen geheim bleiben."

Aus dieser türkischen Antwort geht hervor, wie stark die Türkei daran interessiert war, die sowjetrussische Mit-arbeit bei der Einkreisungsaktion sicherzustellen.[1]

---

[1] Als im Juni 1939 eine türkische Militärmission zu Besprechungen über Kriegsmateriallieferungen in London weilte, berichtete der Delegationsführer General Orbay, dass man angesichts eventueller Schwierigkeiten, das von England zu liefernde Material nach der Türkei zu überführen, in Betracht ziehe, das ganze von England angeforderte Material von Russland zu beziehen. Orbay äusserte ferner, dass England nur einen Teil der türkischen Ansprüche werde befriedigen können, da es den Bedürfnissen und Forderungen des eigenen Heeres und des Heeres der Verbündeten sowie denen der Ostfront gegenüberstehe. (N 121 213)

A typical page from the original German document—the translation of this passage appears on page 60.

Introduction

The document now printed is one of the very few surviving examples of the work of the most secret of all the German intelligence agencies active in the Nazi era, the *Forschungsamt* (Research Office). Very little apart from the fact of its existence appears to have been known by Allied Intelligence agencies during the war. Its own records were in great part destroyed in January 1945 in Breslau to avoid their falling into Russian hands. The office was evacuated to Breslau after its headquarters on the Schillerstrasse in Berlin-Charlottenburg had been burnt out by British incendiaries on the night of 22 November 1943. The remaining records were destroyed at the end of April 1945 before the German capitulation. Its existence was mentioned at the trial of its erstwhile head, Reichs-Marschall Hermann Göring, on war crimes charges at Nuremberg. But it has only received the scantiest of attention by historians and memoir writers since 1945. Yet its intelligence reports, the so-called 'brown pages', *Braune Blätter,* covered the whole range of international and domestic political and economic intelligence. They were circulated to a wide range of German Ministries and other interested agencies. And at the height of its activity it employed well over three thousand people and enjoyed a budget of twenty-five million Reichsmarks.

The job of the *Forschungsamt* was, in the jargon of the intelligence agencies, purely 'passive'; to collect and record information in accordance with general and specific requests made to it by other German Government agencies. Its information came in part from monitoring public sources of information, the foreign press, radio and press services, in part from monitoring radio, wireless, and all telecommunications traffic passing in and out of German-controlled territory. It never employed any agents; and it never planted microphones. It simply listened in to all public forms of communication. A great deal of its work was the provision of economic intelligence, especially after the outbreak of war in 1939, when its information on the movement of world prices, the availability of new material supplies and so on were of considerable importance to the management of Germany's war economy. This was particularly true apparently of the information it provided on the Russian war economy from monitoring official domestic Soviet radio traffic during 1943–4.

On the German domestic front it fulfilled two very different roles. At request it would tap the phones of particular individuals. For example, it is said to have tapped the phone of the Gauleiter of Franconia, the dementedly anti-Semitic Julius Streicher. It listened to the conversations of Unity Mitford, Hitler's most prominent feminine British admirer. It is said to have kept a watch on Hitler's adjutant, Captain Wiedemann, and on the egregious Princess Stefanie von Hohenlohe. It tapped the phone of the film actress, Lida Barova. More importantly it kept a close ear to all the reportage of the foreign diplomats and press representatives in Germany on German conditions, events and morale. And it produced daily reports on foreign propaganda, radio, leaflet or press material directed at Germany.

From this it will be seen that the interception of diplomatic telegraphic correspondence, its deciphering and decoding and the tapping of diplomatic telephones was only one part of its work, though an important part. It is this aspect alone with which the document here reproduced is concerned. It appears to have had considerable success in various directions, if the information on its activities scattered through the surviving German official records is accurate. From the German naval records, for example, it is clear that the French diplomatic code had been broken as early as 1937. For the German naval records make it clear that the French had some information on the outcome of the conference Hitler called on 5 November 1937, to settle a bitter dispute between the three German armed services on the allocation of armour plate. A German intercept of the French embassy's report caused a top-level investigation into the source of the French information, but the source of the leak was not discovered. It was at this conference that Hitler revealed to his military advisers his intention to seize Austria and Czechoslovakia at the first available opportunity; though the French seem only to have been informed of that part of the conference, the tail-end, which covered the allocation of armour plate.

Again in July 1940 when Hitler was pondering in vain why Britain would not accept his offer of peace talks, but preferred to wait for her inevitable devastation from the air and occupation, intercepted telephone conversations were apparently among the factors which convinced him that Britain was relying on the promise of Soviet aid and intervention, and turned his mind like that of Napoleon before him, to the idea that the road to a British defeat lay through Moscow, and revived in him that drive for conquest in the East he had proclaimed in *Mein Kampf* and stifled after Munich to turn against Britain. But the document here printed is of greater historical importance than either of these, since it gives a far wider view of the scope and weaknesses of the German monitoring and cryptographic services.

The record here printed shows that the experts of the *Forschungsamt* were able, in part at least, to read the codes and listen in to telephone conversations between the embassies and legations in Berlin and the foreign offices of Britain, France, Italy, Japan, Turkey, Belgium, Bulgaria, Yugoslavia and Latvia. In addition they benefited from the position of Berlin and Vienna as centres of the European cable system (all cables to Moscow and the Far East ran through Berlin, as those from London to South-East Europe ran through Vienna) to intercept communications between the Japanese embassies in Western Europe and Tokyo, between the Turkish embassy in Moscow and Ankara, and between the Bulgarian and Yugoslav legations in London and Paris and Sofia and Belgrade. There is no evidence that at this date they could read diplomatic codes of the United States; there is equally no evidence that they could not. They certainly 'broke' some American diplomatic codes during the war. They did listen in to the American Minister in Warsaw, Mr Anthony J. Drexel Biddle IV, telephoning an American journalist in London. There is one reference that suggests, but only suggests, that some communication between the Soviet embassy in London and Moscow had been intercepted. But there is a great deal of negative evidence that the general communications of the Soviet diplomatic service were not understood or decipherable to them.

History of the Forschungsamt

Organised and systematic monitoring of radio and telegraphic communications for the purposes of intelligence gathering began in Germany as elsewhere at the time of the first world war. The first office charged with this job was set up in the German Army Supreme Command. It did not survive the German defeat of 1918. In 1921 a new office, the Cypher and Monitoring Office, *Chiffrier und Horchleitstelle*, was established by the German Ministry of Defence as part of the German military intelligence organisation, the *Abwehr*. The *Abwehr* was however concerned solely with military and strategic intelligence, and information on political and economic matters of interest to other government agencies was only passed on intermittently to those whom the office thought might be interested. The result was a proliferation of ministerial intelligence agencies. By 1932 the need for some central intelligence agency was so clear that the officials of the *Chiffrier und Horchleitstelle* proposed that their agency should be separated from the *Abwehr* and become the nucleus of a single government intelligence office attached to the Chancellor's office, and headed by a special commissioner from the highest offices of state. The proposal ran into certain bureaucratic difficulties and was dropped.

Its revival in 1933 after Hitler's advent to power appears to have been inspired by a general agreement among the senior German bureaucrats that such an organisation ought to be set up as soon as possible under their own auspices, otherwise they might well find it being done by the Nazi party. Hitler was apparently unwilling to agree to so great a degree of centralisation, and failed, for once, to see the possibilities of control inherent in the existence of a telephone monitoring agency. He refused to have the agency attached to his own Chancellor's Office, and gave it instead to Göring, his deputy, to be attached to the office of the Minister President of Prussia, a position which Göring combined with that of head of the newly founded German Ministry of Air Transport. Göring placed it under the control of his senior civil servant, State Secretary Körner, and camouflaged it still further by renaming it the Research Office—Ministry of Air Transport. It seems to have retained its monopoly of monitoring telephone, telegraphic and teleprinter communications until early in the war. Otherwise the proliferation of intelligence agencies continued. The new office came into existence on 10 April 1933 under the command of the previous head of the *Chiffrier und Horchleitstelle*, Lieutenant Commander Schimpf. In 1934 it acquired radio monitoring services at Templin and Glienecke, and telephone monitoring offices in Cologne, Nuremberg, Hamburg and Königsberg. A further office in Munich was added in 1935. That same year it moved its headquarters into the offices on the Schillerstrasse it was to continue to occupy until 1943. In 1935 also its first director committed suicide. As his successor Göring appointed Prince Christoph of Hesse.

With the outbreak of war the work of the office was greatly enlarged. New offices were set up in the areas under German occupation. The six original departments became six groups of 15 departments in all and the numbers of staff grew and multiplied. In 1943 Prince Christoph was killed in Italy and succeeded by Ministerial Director Schapper. In November that year, as noted earlier, the office's headquarters were burnt out in a British air raid. An evacuation to Klettersdorf near Breslau was already under preparation; and the main offices and files were now transferred there, leaving only the telephone interception offices and the new director's small personal office in Berlin. New and more spacious offices began to be constructed with feverish haste at Lübben.

All these plans however came to an end with the Soviet invasion of Silesia in January 1945. For lack of transport out of Breslau the vast part of the office's archives was destroyed until only a small part remained to be returned to Berlin. In February a new home was found for the office in Kaufbeuren. A small section remained in Berlin, evacuating the city only on 20 April, and following Admiral Dönitz's staff to Glücksberg in Schleswig-Holstein. There they fell into British hands, and were used for a time (they were a radio monitoring unit) to supply the local commander with news about the progress of the fighting denied him by his superiors. The Kaufbeuren group was officially disbanded on 24 April, all its material and secret documents being destroyed. A small group only of about 100 armed men were evacuated into the Tyrol in search of the Nazis' alpine redoubt. With Göring's arrest on Hitler's instructions on 26 April, the Gauleiter of the Tyrol, Hofer, expelled them. On 30 April 1945, in Stefanskirchen near Rosenheim, in the anti-aircraft barracks that was their last home, this last residue of the *Forschungsamt* was finally disbanded, three days before the barracks fell into American hands.

The Forschungsamt and the Nazis

One of the most surprising aspects of the history of the *Forschungsamt* is that its senior officials, with Göring's backing, managed almost until the end to stay free of Nazi party or police control. Those of its senior officials who survive believe that this was in part due to Hitler's identification of it with the old German bureaucracy which he disliked so much. In part it may well have been fear of the consequences of its falling into the hands of his more ambitious juniors. The Foreign Minister, von Ribbentrop, loathed it as a source of information to Hitler which was outside his control. He made frequent efforts to secure that its reports should only go to Hitler through him. But as a Johnny-come-lately to the Nazi hierarchy he was unable to prevail over Göring's flat refusal. Its cyphering service was at the beginning so much better than his own that he was on occasion reduced to copying the *Forschungsamt's* reports on to white paper and using them as though they came from the Foreign Ministry. Nor can he have been pleased when the *Forschungsamt* pointed out that as they had no difficulty in decoding his radio-telegrams to Japan, they were probably being decoded elsewhere. Early in the war years he set up within the Foreign Ministry a special monitoring unit to concentrate on diplomatic radio and telecommunications, whose reports were circulated as the *Weisse Blätter* (white pages).

Bitterer enemies than von Ribbentrop were, however, to be found in the Gestapo and the S.S. From its earliest days, the Gestapo did its utmost to take the office over. Successive heads of the Gestapo and S.S., Diels, Himmler, Heydrich, Schellenberg, Kaltenbrunner, in turn bombarded Hitler and Göring with the same arguments, alleging that the officials of the *Forschungsamt* were politically unreliable, inefficient and prone to circulate material damaging to official morale and contrary to the Gestapo and S.S. Towards the end the Gestapo began setting up their own telephone taps independently of the *Forschungsamt*. In March 1945 Schellenberg, using the office's own arguments for the need for a single centralised intelligence agency, at last won authorisation to absorb the organisation into the S.S. But even at the end a number of the regional offices had still evaded absorption. The allied occupying authorities in the West recognised this independence of attitude very quickly at the end of the war. Officials of the *Forschungsamt* were absolved of the need to attend denazification courts and exempted from the provisions freezing the property of former Nazis.

The Organisation of the Office

Until 1941, the *Forschungsamt* was organised into six departments. In 1941 these six became departmental groups with fifteen departments divided between them. The six main departments handled organisation, personnel questions, strategy direction, deciphering, evaluation and technical matters. Under these the operating offices were classified as A, B, C, D or F offices. Those offices grouped under the letter A were concerned entirely with the monitoring of telephone communications. Groups B, C and D were concerned with radio communications, wireless broadcasts, and teleprinter and telegraphic communications. The individual offices for telephone monitoring which were placed in fifteen major German cities and in 1942–43 in fifteen major European cities as well carried the cover name 'Research Offices A'. Similar cover names covered the seven offices in Germany and the five outside concerned with monitoring radio communications, including diplomatic and military communications, 'Research Offices B', and the offices concerned with monitoring wireless broadcasts and teleprinter and telegraphic communications. Group F comprised the offices which were engaged in conjunction with the Ministry of Defence in censoring foreign mails. The censorship offices were in fact part of the Ministry of Defence, later the Supreme Command of the Armed Forces (*OKW*). But they included personnel of the *Forschungsamt* concerned not with censorship but the collection of information and intelligence. They were however of comparatively minor importance in the general work of the whole *Forschungsamt* enterprise.

The two key departments in the *Forschungsamt* were those concerned with deciphering and the evaluation of the intelligence collected. The work of the deciphering department in 1933 occupied only six officers dealing with 200–300 items a month. Ten years later there were two hundred and forty employees dealing with three thousand items a month and, at that, the work of the offices suffered from a continuous shortage of qualified personnel. Among other successes they were supplying the Afrika Corps with accurate orders of battle for the Eighth Army, based on their observation of British military radio traffic; the German navy was being regularly supplied with reports on Soviet naval movements in the Baltic; and domestic Soviet radio traffic was providing a mine of information on the Soviet war economy.

But the collection of intelligence is of little value without its proper organisation and evaluation. Here the work of the evaluation department was of the first importance. Until 1941 this department comprised two divisions: Group A was concerned solely with the evaluation of material obtained from the *Forschungsamt's* own various monitoring stations; Group B was concerned with the evaluation of published sources of information, the foreign press being its principal target; though it also kept a close watch on the technical press, as on books, pamphlets and other publications.

The evaluation offices were enjoined to observe the utmost objectivity in their work, as indeed the document here printed, which is an example of the longer memoranda they would produce, clearly demonstrates. It was indeed this objectivity which was most frequently the source of conflict between the *Forschungsamt* and those who felt that the circulation, even within government circles, of information and evaluation they did not themselves control was a threat to their own position if not to morale or public security. They made themselves rather less than popular, for example, by producing in mid-August 1939 a memorandum listing all the evidence that American support would be thrown behind Britain once war broke out, a memorandum which was sent both to von Ribbentrop and Hitler. They were also responsible for the daily circulation of intercepted and monitored material which came to be known as the *Braune Blätter*, 'Brown pages'. Hardly any examples of these have survived. A complete list of those presented to Hitler between 1940 and 1942 is printed in Related Documents I.

The Provenance of the Document

The document here printed comes from the archives of the German Foreign Ministry which fell into the hands of the Western allies in 1945. It was first collected with the other captured archives in Berlin for screening by the historians of the tripartite Anglo-Franco-American project set up to publish the German documents on the origins of the Second World War as part of their determination to prevent any controversy on the responsibility for its outbreak such as that which the Germans and Hitler so skilfully exploited in the 1920s and 1930s. During the Berlin blockade of 1948–49 all these materials were evacuated from Berlin to Britain; and the project continued in the depths of the Buckinghamshire countryside at Whaddon Hall outside Bletchley, where both historians and archives were housed until the return of the archives to the German Federal Republic in 1958–59. During this period this document was recorded on photostat; and the photostat now forms part of the immense collection held by the British Foreign Office Library. The author of this preface saw and inspected the original during this period. The original was part of the collection of German official documents returned to the West German government in 1959, and is to be found in the political archives of the German Foreign Office at Bonn.

In all the document runs to 83 pages, all of them the characteristic brown paper of these reports. It was bound in a separate dark grey cardboard folder and formed part of the collection of files of the Under State Secretary's office. It bears on its first page the name of the Under State Secretary, 'Woermann', and his signature, 'W[oermann]', to mark that he had seen and read it. It clearly did not pass through the normal or even the secret Foreign Ministry registry, since it is quite devoid of file number, stamped date of reception, distribution list or any other indication that anyone but Woermann and the man who wrote his name on it ever saw it. It bears only one official mark on its first page, the typed notation 'U[nder] St[ate Secretary] *Auswärtiges Amt*' (Foreign Ministry), presumably an address typed by the *Forschungsamt*, as it was done on a typewriter with German Gothic type face, a type rarely if ever used in the German Foreign Ministry. It bears on every page the long warning about secrecy here reproduced on page 43 only. This is in fact printed in red on the paper on which the document has been typed or rather mimeographed in blue. In several places the reproduction overlies the printed warning and the top line or lines are difficult to read except on the original .Every page also carries the file number given to the document in the *Forschungsamt*, 'N.140,098'. References in the text show that all *Braune Blätter* based on intercepts were numbered consecutively with a number preceded by the letter N, presumably for N[*achricht*] (information). The numbers run on from year to year (there is a reference to N.71,962 possibly of October 1937, while the last intercepted telephone conversation here, of one p.m. on 3 September 1939, is numbered N.127,344). External evidence suggests that the whole memorandum was issued in about November 1939; and certainly before 11 February 1940, the date of a *Forschungsamt* report seen to be numbered N.150,721 (see Related Documents I, page 124).

The Historical Importance of the Document

This document sets out a picture of British policy towards Germany from the signature of the Munich Agreement to the British declaration of war on Germany at 11 a.m. on 3 September 1939. It is based entirely on two kinds of sources, themselves an odd combination: press reports on the one hand, open to everyone, and intercepted diplomatic telegrams and telephone conversations, available only to the *Forschungsamt* on the other. The unknown author of the document, presumably a member of Department F, evaluation, prefaces his account of the last ten days before the outbreak of war which forms part IV of his work with the statement that he has deliberately refrained from widening the scope of his narrative by using the various 'White Papers' and 'Blue Books' (i.e. the various collections of diplomatic documents on the origins of the war published by the British, French, Polish and German Governments after the outbreak of war). He might have made a similar disclaimer for the other parts of his document. They make it clear that he not only did not consult the 'Coloured Books' produced by the British, French and Polish Governments as well as by the German Government itself; he was either not allowed access to the records of the German Foreign Ministry or deliberately refrained from consulting them.

This comes out particularly strongly in the very patchy nature of the sources used and the picture formed of the negotiations which took place between March and August of 1939 between the British and Soviet Governments for the conclusion of a 'front' against further German aggression, which ended when the Soviet authorities preferred instead to conclude a non-aggression pact with Nazi Germany. It so happens that the German embassy in London on several occasions had very rapid and accurate information on the secret exchanges between London and Moscow, information which suggests, to say the least, indiscretion from a very well-informed source on the British side. On two occasions, the information was given to them the same day. (The interested reader may care to compare the record of the negotiations in the months April–June 1939 as contained in volumes V and VI of Sir Llewellyn Woodward's publication from the British Foreign Office archives, *Documents on British Foreign Policy, 1919–1939*, 3rd series, with that contained in volume VI of the publication of the tripartite project of selected German Foreign Ministry Records, *Documents on German Foreign Policy, 1918–1945*, Series D, paying special attention to documents Nos. 201 and 520 in volume V and 35 in volume VI of the former with documents Nos. 239, 381 and 511 in the latter. The series are available in most good public central and university libraries.) Yet is it clear that the *Forschungsamt* were nothing like so well informed.

In this the *Forschungsamt* were presumably just ill-informed. In another very important instance they were a good deal less than candid. This is in the matter of the negotiations conducted between their head, Field Marshal Göring, and the British, via the Swedish businessman, Birger Dahlerus, in the month of August 1939. Herr Dahlerus who was unkindly, though not unfairly, dubbed by that most masterly of British diplomatic historians, the late Sir Lewis Namier, an 'interloper in diplomacy' was on several occasions appallingly indiscreet when telephoning London from the private flat of the British Ambassador in Berlin, Sir Nevile Henderson. Indeed he was so indiscreet on the afternoon of 31

August, that his collocutor in London was finally obliged to break the connection, having failed entirely to induce him to talk more discreetly. Lord Halifax was driven to address a letter of remonstrance to Henderson that same day. It is clear from numerous references in the last part of this document that Henderson's private phone had a regular tap on it; but there is no mention of the incident whatever in this document. Göring hated the Nazi Foreign Minister, Joachim von Ribbentrop, whom he blamed for misleading Hitler as to Britain's alleged unwillingness to go to war. And having failed to keep secret an earlier set of negotiations with the British, conducted by an official of his Four Year Plan organisation, Herr Wohltat, in June and July (also unmentioned in this document), he must have been determined to keep all mention of the Dahlerus negotiations out of a document which might fall into von Ribbentrop's hands. Surviving members of the *Forschungsamt* have testified to the fact that the Dahlerus negotiations were monitored by their offices.

The historical importance of this document can be discussed under two headings; firstly, the contribution it makes as a survey, based on a wide variety of diplomatic materials not otherwise available to the historian, of the events leading up to the outbreak of the Second World War; and, secondly, the attention it focuses on that little known dimension, the role of secret intelligence in the vital decisions of recent history. The one is general, the other particular. The one illuminates our picture of British policy; the other bears on the reasoning behind German policy.

The Forschungsamt picture of British policy

This document makes two main contributions to our understanding of British policy in the months before the outbreak of war. In the first place it fills in the picture of and underlines the importance of British policy in South East Europe in the months between March and August 1939. Although most of the events here dealt with are covered by the published British documents there has been a tendency to see them very much in compartments from the viewpoint of the actual outcome of the year, the German attack on Poland. Thus the British guarantees to Rumania and Poland on the one hand and to Turkey and Greece on the other are seen as separate and distinct reactions to the successive moves by Germany in occupying what was left of Czechoslovakia after

Munich and following that a few days later by the occupation of Memel and the Italian aggression against Albania on Good Friday; and British policy towards Greece and Turkey is seen essentially as reactions to the second, Italian, move, rather than a logical development from the actually mistaken assumption that the two dictators were acting in collusion with one another. The British negotiations with the Soviet Union are seen essentially therefore as an outcrop of the guarantee for Poland, aimed at securing a degree of Soviet support without which the guarantee was impossible to fulfil and therefore lacking in credibility. As a result the British line in the negotiations with the Soviet Union has always seemed to fall so determinedly short of what the situation seemed to require as to invite speculation as to the stupidity or general malevolence towards the Soviet Union of those who originated it. It seems so obvious that the Soviet Union was the only power capable of intervening militarily to aid Poland against a German invasion, that the apparent unwillingness of the British government to accept a Soviet military alliance has only been explicable on the assumption either that the British could not recognise the military realities of the situation, and were therefore criminally stupid, or that they did recognise them, and hoped to lure the Soviet Union into a unilateral guarantee of Poland which would so engage Germany and the Soviet Union in military conflict as to weaken, if not to destroy, them both.

What this document does in its approach and structure is to remind us that this was not actually how things happened. Britain's alarm was first aroused by the actions of the Rumanian Minister in London, M. Tilea. The circumstances of the alarm focused attention first of all on the Balkans and the key position of Turkey. The guarantee for Poland was an interpolation into the course of British policy brought about by a quite unnecessary panic that German action against Danzig and the Corridor was imminent. German-Polish negotiations had in fact just broken down. But the military orders to prepare for an attack on Poland were not issued until 3 April, three days after the British guarantee. And the main weight of British diplomacy was still directed towards creating a solid bloc of powers in South East Europe which would stand in the way of any further Axis expansion. It was no accident that the guarantees to Rumania and Greece were given on the same day, 13 April 1939, or that such great encouragement was given to Turkey and to Turkish diplomacy among the other three members of the Balkan Entente, Rumania, Greece and Yugoslavia, to bring them together with their arch enemy, Bulgaria, in a bloc which Germany could clearly only tackle by outright military aggression.

M. Tilea's action, and the erroneous assumption that Hitler and Mussolini were acting in collusion, thus set British policy slightly aslant of what was to be Hitler's main direction of aggression, against Poland alone. If one assumes that the main aim of British policy was to defend Poland against Germany then the policy followed towards the Soviet Union is legitimately open to criticism. If one assumes however that the aim of British policy was to produce a united front in South and South Eastern Europe, to be guaranteed by Britain and France with the Soviet Union as a kind of long-stop, as a means of 'containing' Hitler prior to negotiating with him 'from strength', then it makes more sense and one can see where it broke down, on the failure to conciliate Bulgaria and the pitiful wobbling of the Rumanian Government.

This document, drawing on Bulgarian and Yugoslav intercepts, depicts the British as more actively engaged in pressure on Bulgaria than the few scattered documents in the official British publications suggest. These latter show rather the British leaving the initiative to Turkey and Rumania, while pressing them to take it. Their picture is in part confirmed by the absence of any serious reference to diplomatic activity in the summer of 1939 in the memoirs of the British Minister in Sofia at that time, Mr George Rendel, whose memoirs at other places are quite informative.

In concentrating on British policy in the Balkans and examining in turn its reflection in negotiations with Rumania, Bulgaria, Greece, Turkey and Yugoslavia (but not, curiously, Hungary), the document brings out very strongly the importance in the British plan of Turkey, and the importance to Turkey of a successful outcome of the Anglo-Soviet negotiations. This is in itself of extreme importance. But that is not all, since it is suggestive in its report (on page 71) of Anglo-Turkish and Anglo-Soviet discussions of the possible entry of British warships into the Black Sea through the Dardanelles. From the British record it would appear that this report is mistaken. But it focuses attention again on the question of Soviet anxieties as to the control of the Dardanelles which had passed irretrievably under Turkish control by the Convention of Montreux in 1936 with British support, against the bitter objections of the Soviet delegation. Between 1936 and 1939 Anglo-Turkish relations had become steadily closer; and one is left wondering how the Soviet authorities can have viewed the British efforts to construct a unified bloc of states in the Balkans with active Turkish participation, and themselves relegated to the position of absentee, non-participating guarantor.

The account of the origins of the Rumanian action here given under-lines still further the element of chance and misapprehension in the formulation of British policy. There has always been an element of mystery in M. Tilea's dramatic appearance in the Foreign Office on 17 March 1939, two days after the German annexation of Bohemia, with talk of an ultimatum being issued by Germany in the current economic negotiations in Bucharest. His intervention was almost immediately disowned by his government; and it is difficult to find any trace of an ultimatum in the German records of these conversations. According to the Rumanian historian, V. Mosiuc, the instructions on which Tilea acted and his own record of the conversations he held have no reference to any German ultimatum. He was however instructed to do his utmost to secure a positive British policy in South East Europe, and he did tell the British that his government had reason to fear that they might be the next victim of German aggression. It is thus extremely useful to have the Yugoslav record cited here on p. 62 confirming that Tilea did speak of an 'economic ultimatum'; that he did tell his Yugoslav colleague in London that the Rumanian Government had used the German demands to increase the general tension and to secure Rumania's security against every eventuality; and that he had made the 'utmost possible use of his instructions'. One must conclude that he had; that he succeeded in dup-ing the whole British government; and that the episode as here, and elsewhere, recorded throws into stark relief the occasional lapses into total panic of which the Foreign Office, at first sight so Olympian, and its still more Olympian political head, Lord Halifax, were capable.

The other major contribution this document makes to our under-standing of the period is in the detailed picture it gives of the diplomatic activity in Berlin during the last ten days of peace. It cannot be said that the British Ambassador, Sir Nevile Henderson, emerges with any real credit from its picture of his agitated telephoning or the violent row he apparently had with his French colleague, M. Coulondre, on the even-ing of 31 August, about the Polish unwillingness to take up the German offer to discuss their proposals in Berlin with a Polish plenipotentiary without having received any formal statement or invitation from the German Government; and his frenzied clutching the next day at the idea of a meeting at the end of the eleventh hour between the Polish

Commander in Chief, General Rydz-Smigly, and Field Marshal Göring does little credit to his grasp of realities. It is interesting to observe the attitude of optimism which spread in London on 26 and 27 August, presumably as a result of their knowledge that Hitler had cancelled the orders for an attack on Poland at dawn on 26 August, as a result of the Italian defection from the Axis alliance and the signature of Britain's alliance with Poland. The picture of the general comings and goings within the diplomatic community in Berlin adds a good deal too to the general picture we have of that community and its reactions under stress, something which appears all too rarely from the cold prose of the official documents or the justificatory passages of the various ambassadorial memoirs.

The questionable security of British communications

The amount of information on British policy in this document must inevitably raise two questions in the reader's mind: firstly, how secure were British diplomatic communications in this period from German penetration, and, secondly, what effect did the knowledge of British moves contained in these documents have on German policy.

The evidence in this document shows that the Germans had only in part penetrated the British diplomatic ciphers. On a number of important matters where one would expect a full knowledge of the diplomatic codes to have given them adequate information, their account is simply wrong. Their account of the origins of the British guarantee to Greece (p. 65) is quite wrong. So is their account (p. 77) of the origins of the visit paid to London by Colonel Beck, the Polish Foreign Minister, on 4–6 April, and their account (p. 78) of the origins of the British guarantee to Poland.

Then they are wrong on a number of dates and timings. They have Chamberlain addressing the Commons on a date it was not in session (p. 49). They have Sir Nevile Henderson complaining of the activities of the British press by telegram from Berlin at a date when he was in London (p. 88). They have Henderson's actions on the morning of 30 August wrong (p. 102) and the hour of his midnight visit to von Ribbentrop that night quite wrong. They also have the instructions which passed between London and Berlin earlier that evening post-timed by at least an hour.

They are also remarkably ill-informed on certain points. The contrast between their ignorance of the course of the Anglo-Soviet negotiations and the accuracy of the information reaching the German Embassy in London has already been mentioned. They were far from accurately informed about the course of the Anglo-Polish or Anglo-Turkish negotiations. They connected the visit of Mr Strang and Mr Jebb of the Foreign Office to Warsaw at the end of May 1939 with preparations for the signature of the Anglo-Polish alliance (p. 80) whereas it appears to have been a simple visit of information. They depict the Turks as receiving arms from Britain in 'vast amounts' and at an 'accelerated rate' (p. 61) at a time when the Turks were complaining bitterly that they were not getting any war material whatever from Britain. Their misinformation on the Dardanelles issue has already been mentioned. They were also under the illusion (p. 70) that the Anglo-Soviet talks were covering the Far East.

None of this suggests a complete mastery of the British codes and ciphers. True, they refer in detail to a number of British notes to the German Government, including one hitherto quite unknown message from Chamberlain to Hitler on 5 October 1938, pleading for a favourable reference to his contacts with Hitler to be included in the speech to be made by Hitler that evening, to support Chamberlain in his efforts to give a lead to British opinion. These would however have been sent, in normal diplomatic practice, either *en clair* or in a very simple code, since otherwise one would simply be handing over to opponents a literal key to one's more secret ciphers. This would presumably also apply to the British communications of 11 November 1938 and 14 and 17 March 1939 (pp. 51, 52 and 53).

A further indication that the German decipherers were by no means privy to the full range of British ciphers can be found in their references to a British warning to Germany, given on 11 May, that a German attack on Poland would bring into operation the British and French guarantees (p. 80). The British documents make it plain that instructions to speak in this sense to the German Foreign Ministry were, in fact, sent to Henderson on 11 May. But they were sent, at Henderson's own request, as a warning to the Germans in a cipher the Germans were believed to have broken. (Apparently the fact that this particular cipher was insecure had been revealed to the British authorities the previous year by a member of the German underground.) The precise point of this manoeuvre is a little obscure; but the references in the published British Foreign Office documents make it quite clear that this is, in fact, what happened.

The *Forschungsamt* report here printed tends to suggest that other British ciphers must have been compromised by the degree to which the British embassy in Berlin relied on the telephone as a means of exchanging urgent telegrams with London. For example, we find Sir Nevile Henderson dictating to the Embassy in Berlin the text of a telegram to London giving his first, extremely gloomy impressions of his visit to Berchtesgaden on 23 August to hand over to Hitler the text of a letter from the Prime Minister (p. 93). The *Forschungsamt's* text is virtually identical with the text of the Embassy's telegram to London, printed in *Documents on British Foreign Policy*, 3rd Series, volume VII, as document No. 502. But the British Foreign Office records show that the telegram was in fact sent *en clair*. A similar case is that of Henderson's telegram of 2 September on his midnight visit to von Ribbentrop on 30 August, which this report again carries in direct quotation. (Compare the text here printed, on p. 104, with the text in *D.B.F.P.*, vol. VII, document 715). This too was sent *en clair*. So too was his urgent telegram of 31 August on the German demand that the Polish ambassador in Berlin, Josef Lipski, should at once be empowered to negotiate with them (pp. 105–06). In this case however the German version differs in one significant instance from that printed in the British documents (*D.B.F.P.*, vol. VII, No. 577), in representing Henderson as adding that the Germans might be bluffing. A further case is that of a second telegram of 31 August cited verbatim (p. 106) on the same point (*D.B.F.P., Vol.* XII, No. 582) which again on enquiry turns out to have been sent *en clair*.

The British Embassy staff were far from discreet however in their use of the telephone for direct conversation with one another within Berlin or with London on procedural matters. Cases in point are the conversation held by Mr Holman early on 30 August (p. 101) and the Foreign Office's communication with Sir Nevile Henderson that same afternoon (pp. 102–03), which does not appear in *D.B.F.P.*, vol. VII. Perhaps the most indiscreet of all Henderson's telephone conversations however were those he undertook in the early hours of 31 August. He had in fact just been visited by the Italian Ambassador, Bernard Attolico, and by the former German Ambassador in Rome, Ulrich von Hassell, already a confirmed anti-Nazi, doomed to be executed by the S.S. for his part in the conspiracy to assassinate Hitler which so narrowly failed on 20 July 1944. They came with information originally provided by the State Secretary in the German Foreign Ministry, von Weizsäcker, that a German attack on Poland was imminent. Henderson repeated their information on the telephone not once but three times, to the Secretary of the Polish Embassy in Berlin, to the Foreign Office in London, and to his French colleague in Berlin, M. Robert Coulondre—all within an hour of von Hassell's clandestine visit to him. Such neglect of the security of his informant in a police state is truly remarkable. It leaves one with the feeling that the Germans did not need a key to the British ciphers. They only needed to lure Sir Nevile Henderson to the telephone.

The general lack of security in the British diplomatic service

Sir Nevile Henderson's indiscretions are however uncharacteristic of the British foreign service as a whole at this period. The *Forschungsamt*, impressed by the normal discipline at the telephone observed by his colleagues, thought many of his indiscretions were deliberate. But the lack of proper security screening procedure in the British Foreign Service had already led to its being penetrated by Donald Maclean, then in the British Embassy in Paris. There would appear to have been both an Italian and a Soviet agent, or alternatively one shared between the Italian and Soviet Embassies in London, firmly ensconced in the Foreign Office's Archives Section. Though perhaps the most extraordinary case of lack of security seems to have occured in the British Embassy in Rome where from mid-1935 until the Italian entry into the war against Britain in 1940, the British Embassy safe was regularly burgled once a week and all new confidential material regularly copied. According to Sir Robert, later Lord, Vansittart, the British Ambassador, Lord Perth, refused to take any measures to improve security even when Lady Perth's tiara was removed by the thief, a professional burglar in the pay of the Italian intelligence authorities. With a remarkable sense of business the thief also sold copies of all he removed from the British Embassy to the Soviet Embassy in Rome. The Italians were thus of a certainty in possession of all the diplomatic codes and ciphers used in the British diplomatic service, though they did not in fact pass them on to the Germans until after their entry into the war in 1940.

How far were the British uncharacteristic in this
lack of security?

In justice to the British it must however be noted that Sir Nevile Henderson was not unique in his indiscreet use of the telephone. The record
here printed shows that his colleagues in Berlin were equally indiscreet,
especially M. Coulondre, the French Ambassador and Signor Attolico,
the Italian representative. In view of the use made by the Italians of
telephone tapping and cipher-breaking techniques, one would have
expected that their own diplomatic service would have been particularly
cautioned against indiscreet use of the telephone; but the record here
printed shows that if any such instructions were given they were ignored.
Only the Russians and the Americans seem to have shown reasonable
security on the line. In the *Forschungsamt's* own reckoning the Russians
and the Japanese were totally secure in their use of the telephone. They
reckoned the British and American record of security on the phone to
be good, whereas the Italians, French, Belgians, Dutch and Balkan
diplomats observed no discipline whatever in their use of the telephone.

This question must raise a second one. How effective were the intelligence activities in this field of other countries known to have been
in this period? The evidence available is scanty and scattered, and must in
part be based on inference rather than certainty. Let us begin with
Britain itself. The activities of agencies equivalent to the *Forschungsamt*
in Britain have been very much veiled since the revelations of the
effectiveness with which they operated during the First World War when
their interception and subsequent publication of the famous Zimmer-
mann telegram of 1917, by which the German Ambassador in Mexico
City was instructed to offer Mexico inducements to attack the United
States, played a considerable part in the events which led up to the
American declaration of war on Germany. Care is taken that no direct
record of their activities survives in the papers which are released to the
Public Records Office for scholarly scrutiny. Various indirect indications
in the published diplomatic documents and elsewhere however suggest
that the Japanese diplomatic code presented them with few problems.
They could, on German evidence, read the Italian naval cipher at the
time of clandestine Italian submarine attacks on merchant shipping in
the Mediterranean in 1937. In 1939 they received from Polish Military
Intelligence keys and machines for decoding German official military

and diplomatic ciphers; they are known to have exchanged a set of such machines in 1941 with the United States, obtaining in return one of the four American machines capable of decoding *Purple*, the top-priority Japanese diplomatic code, which, after eighteen to twenty months work, the Americans had succeeded in cracking in August 1940. The Tyler Kent case in 1940 revealed that they were in fact providing signal facilities for the American Embassy in London for communication with Washington, a circumstance which has led some American writers to voice the suspicion that they did not scruple to read American diplomatic communications. There have also been rumours current at various times that British cryptographers were able to monitor Soviet diplomatic traffic in 1939 and were thus aware of the closeness of Nazi-Soviet contacts, but that, as with the American decipherment of *Purple*, the information derived from this was confined to so small a circle for security reasons that no use could be made of it even within the Foreign Office or in correspondence between the Office and British missions abroad.

The effectiveness of the Italian agencies in this field has never been revealed, nor that of the Soviets. The Americans built up a highly efficient system during and after the First World War, the so-called 'Black Chamber'. It was however disbanded in 1929 in somewhat obscure circumstances by the then Secretary of State, Mr Stimson, on the grounds that 'gentlemen' did not eavesdrop. Revived in the late 1930s it succeeded again in cracking the Japanese military and diplomatic ciphers, though the arrangements for the rapid processing and distribution of the information received did not, as is known, prove adequate to give the American military authorities in Pearl Harbour adequate warning of the impending attack upon them. (The general vulnerability of the Japanese ciphers is so striking that one wonders whether there is something inherent in the Japanese language which prevents its encipherment into any of the more complicated forms of cipher employed by other great powers.) The French Military Intelligence Service, the *Service des Renseignements*, obtained from an employee of the *Forschungsamt* documents which enabled them to reconstruct the cipher machine used by the German military. Unlike the Poles, they do not seem to have communicated this information to their British allies. But, as Mrs Wohlstetter has shown in her brilliant study of the American failure to use the advantages won by their cryptographers to anticipate the Japanese attack on Pearl Harbour, the really important aspect of the role of intelligence in influencing foreign policy is the evaluation and use made of the intelligence once it has been gained.

The impact of intelligence on German Foreign Policy

The question how one assesses the role secret intelligence plays and played in the process by which statesmen and national leaders reach their decisions is one that has always vexed historians though they have devoted little enough discussion to the problem it presents. The most detailed general discussion of the question was published by the editor-in-chief of the Italian diplomatic documents, Professor Mario Toscano, in 1950. In a paper presented to the Ninth Congress of the Historical Sciences in Paris, he listed five major cases in which the passage of information obtained by secret intelligence agencies could be shown to have had a considerable effect on the policies pursued in specific matters by the governments served by these agencies. Perhaps the most interesting cases he quotes are those where the possession of secret intelligence actually had a deleterious effect on those who received it. In the case of Mussolini, the effectiveness of whose intelligence service's surveillance of the correspondence between the British Foreign Ministry and the embassy in Rome has already been mentioned, his impulsiveness, his sensitivity to what he took to be personal slights, and the degree to which he saw Italy's role in foreign affairs as an aspect of the manifestations of his own personality and prestige inhibited, indeed often paralysed, his native sense of realism. The insults with which in the year 1937 his tame press and radio pursued Mr Eden, the Foreign Secretary, within weeks of the signature of the so-called Gentlemen's Agreement between Italy and Britain, were a direct reaction to the anti-Italian sentiments expressed by Eden in correspondence with the various British diplomatic missions in the Balkans instructing them to try to nerve the governments to which they were accredited to withstand Italian pressure.

Another case in point is the influence of the Soviet spy ring in Tokyo headed by the German, Richard Sorge. From the information he and his Japanese associate, Ozaki, obtained from Ozaki's position in the Japanese Cabinet Office and from Sorge's friends in the German Embassy in Tokyo, where he was a greatly valued adviser on Japanese affairs, the Soviet authorities were immediately informed of the contents of the secret protocol to the German-Japanese anti-Comintern pact of

November 1936. And they knew that the highly secret negotiations to turn this pact into a military alliance, conducted in the winter of 1938–39 between von Ribbentrop, the Nazi Foreign Minister, and General Oshima, the Japanese Ambassador in Berlin, were intended by the Germans to be directed not against them but against Britain and the United States, from the detailed information on the fruitless attempts by the Japanese Admiralty and Foreign Ministry to get German agreement to the pact being limited to the Soviet Union, provided to them by Sorge. They were thus able to react to German activity in Europe and to the British attempt to gain their support for a front to contain German expansion without any fear of their being next in line for German attack. The policy they followed in the spring and summer of 1939 with their ultimate rejection of the British connection in favour of a pact with Nazi Germany cannot but have owed a great deal to the absence of any real fear of German intentions.

These are two cases in which Sorge's information would seem to have had a very considerable influence on the formation of Soviet foreign policy. The third case, in 1941, underlines the peculiar nature of the difficulty we have in assessing the influence of secret intelligence on the formulation of policy. In 1941, according to the most recent Soviet studies of the Sorge case, Richard Sorge sent an urgent warning of the German plans to attack the Soviet Union. It was dismissed by Stalin as another example of the attempts by British propaganda to ease German pressure on herself by stirring up trouble between Germany and the Soviet Union, and dismissed as worthless. The information did not square with the Soviet leader's convictions and he therefore ignored it. And the German attack on the Soviet Union on 22 June 1941 came as a complete strategic surprise to Stalin and his government.

This last example must bear very heavily on our attempts to assess how the activities of the *Forschungsamt* as revealed in this document had on the policy produced by Germany. The first thing to remember is that under the Nazi regime it is always very dangerous to talk as if there was a single unified policy being pursued by all the various individuals and agencies. For the purpose of this assessment we have to concern ourselves with four different policies, that pursued by Hitler, that advocated by von Ribbentrop, his Foreign Minister, that followed by the professionals of the Foreign Ministry led by the State Secretary, Ernst von Weizsäcker, and finally that followed by the *Forschungsamt's* actual boss, Göring. This is particularly important in view of the rivalry between von Ribbentrop and Göring and their very differing assessments of how Britain would react to a German attack on Poland. It is difficult to believe that Göring provided von Ribbentrop, his detested rival, with much useful *Forschungsamt* material. Ribbentrop had, in any case, a very limited desire to read such material. On the other hand it would be quite probable that Göring would see that copies got to the hands of senior Foreign Ministry officials, with whom he was always on excellent terms. One must assume too that he used or showed this material to Hitler.

It is at this point that the peculiar difficulties of using this kind of material intervene. We have little or no idea how regularly Göring saw Hitler during this period, or what arrangements were made for the submission to Hitler of the intercepts, the *Braune Blätter*. We do not know how long it took the *Forschungsamt* experts to decode the material which fell into their hands or how quickly they put the results of their researches into circulation. One can only compare what they can be shown from this document to have intercepted with Hitler's and Göring's moves in the field of foreign policy, and note any suggestive correlations.

This process reveals three very interesting connections. The first of these concerns the *Forschungsamt's* readings of the policy pursued by the British representative on the international commission charged with overseeing the application and execution of the Munich agreements (p. 49). The author of this survey is of the opinion that these intercepts showed that Britain was still, despite Munich and the Anglo-German declaration, determined to pursue an independent policy in Europe; further that she was trying to inhibit and complicate the execution of the Munich agreement. This is backed by a list of six references, including one to a telephone conversation between Mr Ivone Kirkpatrick of the British Embassy in Berlin and the Foreign Office, two to telephone conversations held between the French ambassador, then M. André François-Poncet, and officials of the Quai d'Orsay in Paris and two to conversations, presumably also on the telephone, between M. François-Poncet and his British colleague, Sir Nevile Henderson.

The interesting point here is not that this impression was justified. The official British documents show that it was quite erroneous. But we know from other sources that Hitler was peculiarly incensed against Britain in this period. A lot of this had to do with the speeches of the British opponents of the Munich agreement, especially Eden and Duff

Cooper, in the Commons debate of 3 October 1938. A lot of it too can be traced to his apparent feeling that in the eyes of the world, including those of a great part of the German people, Munich was Neville Chamberlain's triumph, not his. But one is left with the strong suggestion that these intercepts, in which, it is to be noted, French reports played a far larger role than British, must have played a part in incensing his animosity against Britain still further. One wonders just what M. François-Poncet was saying—even whether he knew or guessed he was being overheard and was taking advantage of his listeners.

The second of these connections is perhaps at once the most interesting and the most speculative. Reference has been made earlier to the differing policies pursued in the summer of 1939 by von Ribbentrop and Göring, and their differing assessments of British determination not to abandon the efforts to restrain Hitler at the brink of war. Göring's conviction that the British were prepared for war as the last resort if Hitler actually attacked Poland led him to promote the clandestine negotiations with the British government for which Herr Birger Dahlerus was the intermediary: he seems to have been aiming for some Munich-style settlement which would obviate once again the need for war. Hitler, however, preferred to believe von Ribbentrop's assurances that Britain would withdraw at the last moment. The question is when Göring formed his conviction that Britain would fight if needs be, and what evidence, what considerations, led him to this view. For Göring was not an indecisive man, nor one so cautious as always to withdraw from taking major risks. And although he seems to have shared the general view of those who served as regular officers in the German forces in 1914–18 that in any war in which Britain and Germany were on opposite sides, the German side would be the loser, he would not have been against taking a risk on Poland if he had been as convinced that the odds were against a British intervention as Hitler was.

Could it be that one of the elements in forming Göring's conviction was the knowledge of these intercepts? If one accepts this possibility, then the section of this report which deals with the swing of British opinion against Germany *before* the German occupation of Prague (p. 50) seems particularly significant. So do the misjudgements of the progress of the Anglo-Polish and Anglo-Turkish talks on arms deliveries mentioned above. Göring could well have seen the British moves to create a Balkan front against further German expansion as a logical development of the increasing British suspicion of Germany already demonstrated in the material produced by the *Forschungsamt* to be in full swing before 15 March 1939. These intercepts, when taken with the fake *démarche* of 11 May 1939, may very well have played an important part in leading Göring to pursue a separate policy tending towards the evidence of a confrontation with Britain, a policy expressed firstly in the encouragement he gave to the initiative taken by his deputy, Wohltat, in opening conversations with Sir Horace Wilson and Robert Hudson, M.P. in June and July 1939, and, when these failed because of von Ribbentrop's intervention, in supporting the initiative taken by Dahlerus in early August 1939.

The influence these intercepts had on Hitler is altogether more difficult to assess when one moves into the period of May–August 1939. The personnel of the *Forschungsamt* themselves were never very clear in their own minds about Hitler's attitude to them. They believed him to be generally hostile to the work of their organisation, through a dislike of their political objectivity and their escape from absorption by the Nazi party. Their main source for this view of Hitler's attitude came from his personal adjutant, Julius Schaub; Schaub is remembered during August 1939 as commenting that Hitler completely rejected the 'pessimistic material of the *Forschungsamt*', showing the probability of British and French intervention in a German-Polish conflict as it 'disturbed the formation of his intuition'. He certainly took little or no interest in their activities or in following up any of the information that reached him from them. The truth is probably that in this period he was so set on war with Poland that he was not prepared to listen to anything that might controvert his decision. His distrust of professional expertise, so apparent in his general attitude to his professional military and diplomatic advisers, would have reinforced him in this rejection, which was supported by von Ribbentrop's continual insistence that Britain and France were bluffing. Thus signs of a weakening in French morale which the *Forschungsamt* claimed to have detected in conversations between the French Embassy and Paris, and of Polish dilatoriness detected in similar telephone communications between Warsaw and the Polish Embassy in Berlin probably were used to confirm his prejudices, while the other evidence was dismissed. He was amply confirmed in his prejudices by von Ribbentrop, whose antipathy to Göring and to the office whose output infringed his monopoly as Foreign Minister has already been mentioned.

The conclusion must be that in this respect the *Forschungsamt's* influence was as unsuccessful as that of Sorge on Stalin in 1941 or the American cryptographers on Roosevelt and Hull that same year. The warnings were given; but they were not heeded. And Hitler stumbled into a war with Britain which he had always advised his military he could well avoid, since the British position was not serious. The official German interpreter, Paul Otto Schmidt, who actually received from Sir Nevile Henderson's hands the text of the British ultimatum on the morning of 3 September 1939, has testified to the effect this had on Hitler; but on the evidence in this document his surprise was not the result of any failure on the part of professional German intelligence, just as it was not for lack of any official warning from the British government, or his own Foreign Ministry officials or his Italian allies. He did not believe because his intuition was otherwise, and Ribbentrop, his jackal, feared to lose position if he gave the lie to his master. Yet Hitler's intuition, so accurate against the prophets of gloom in 1936 at the time of the reoccupation of the Rhineland or even the previous year, in the crisis over Czechoslovakia, had betrayed him. The way was open for the greater misjudgements of 1940, 1941 and 1942 and the inevitable destruction of the Nazi Reich they entailed.

German Cryptographic and Monitoring Agencies during the War Years

This document gives us then a reasonable picture of the work of the *Forschungsamt* up to the outbreak of war. During the war years it was to enjoy very considerable success; at the same time its monopoly position was obviously impossible to maintain. The exigencies of military intelligence demanded a vast increase in the monitoring of enemy military radio traffic; at the same time, the Foreign Ministry, the Reich's Security Headquarters under Himmler, Heydrich and Schellenberg invaded the field. Under the direction of its ambitious Nazi chief, Dr Ohnesorge, the Post Office emerged from passive co-operation with the *Forschungsamt* to active competition. The available evidence is very far from allowing a complete picture to be built up of the extent and scope of this competition. But from various sources, including a list kept by Walther Hewel (the Foreign Office liaison officer at Hitler's headquarters) of the various intercepted intelligence reports submitted to Hitler in the years 1940–42, the following picture can be discerned.

The main field of competition developed was that of monitoring radio communications. Here the most significant units involved were those of the Supreme Command of the Armed Forces (*OKW*), the Foreign Ministry and the Post Office. A document of 1944 lists three agencies as active in the general field: The *Reichspost* Central Office which monitored postal radio services all round the radio dial, as well as radio broadcasts; the *Forschungsamt*, responsible for monitoring political and economic wireless communications of foreign countries; and the Foreign Ministry (Office *Personelle Z*), responsible for monitoring diplomatic wireless communications of foreign countries. In addition there were five purely military monitoring services: the *OKW*, known as the *Chi[ffrier]* Office, responsible for monitoring diplomatic and other international wireless communications in co-operation with the Foreign Ministry; separate services for the army, navy and air forces engaged in monitoring the radio traffic of the respective services of their enemies, and a second *OKW* office charged with monitoring the use of radio by foreign intelligence services operating in and out of Germany.

The Hewel document shows that the bulk of the material submitted to Hitler came from the *Forschungsamt* and the Foreign Ministry. Up to March 1941, the *Forschungsamt* submitted much more material. But after the explosion of Hitler's fury at the Foreign Ministry's failure to give advance warning of the coup d'état in Yugoslavia in March 1941 which overthrew the pro-German Government, the Foreign Ministry greatly stepped up the numbers of intercepts sent to Hitler. Among the ciphers broken in this period by the two offices were those of Spain, Vichy France, Ireland, Egypt, Iran, Sweden, Switzerland, Portugal, and the Free Polish regime in London. More important was their ability from summer 1940 to read various American diplomatic codes. In 1940 one finds messages to Roosevelt from Admiral Leahy, the American representative in Vichy France. In 1941 regular communications between Washington and the American Embassies in Moscow, Ankara, Helsinki, Algiers and Budapest are being read. The travels of Colonel Donovan founder of the American intelligence agency, the Office of Strategic Services, are carefully followed. The same year one finds British communications with their missions in Ankara, and Teheran being regularly submitted to Hitler. In 1942 British circular dispatches, sent for information to Rhodesia, the Congo and other African countries, appear on the list.

But the most successful coup was that scored by the German Post Office whose research office succeeded in March 1942 in breaking the

Scrambler Code used on the radio telephone link between Britain and the United States. It was from this source that in the summer of 1943 the Germans intercepted a conversation between Roosevelt and Churchill which made it clear that the Italians were secretly negotiating an armistice with Britain and the United States, and to take measures to forestall the Allied attempts to exploit the Italian surrender. A large number of British prisoners of war in Italian hands were taken over by the Germans before their release could be effected.

In this the *Forschungsamt* must appear rather out of things. Its major coups were however only very little less in degree. In April 1940 they intercepted a report of the Finnish Minister in Paris of an indiscretion by Paul Reynaud, the French premier, which gave the Germans accurate warning of the British plan to mine Norwegian territorial waters. They obtained from the radio traffic of the French Underground in 1944 an accurate knowledge of the coded warnings to be employed to herald the allied landing in France, for D-Day in fact, and gave the German headquarters in France warning of the impending attack within minutes of the warnings being broadcast. They even claim to have monitored the British diplomatic traffic between London and Moscow in 1942 and to have read some of the Churchill–Stalin correspondence in that year. And during all this period they remained remarkably secure, being penetrated neither by the Nazi party, S.S. or Gestapo, nor by the agents of any foreign power. In February 1944 the head of the section concerned with the evaluation of foreign information on Germany's domestic situation was arrested by the Gestapo and subsequently shot for passing information to a member of the German Secret Service, the *Abwehr*, at a time when the Gestapo were closing in on those members of the *Abwehr* who were using it as a cover for their underground work against Nazism. Only in the last stages of defeat did they, or rather individual units, succumb to the power of the S.S.

D. C. WATT
London School of Economics and Political Science

Christmas 1967

N140098

Zu der englischen Politik
vom Münchner Abkommen bis zum Kriegsausbruch
===

Gl Zo TF/Ne Mn Kl

Vst. Auswärtiges - Amt

N 140098

ON BRITISH POLICY FROM MUNICH
TO THE OUTBREAK OF WAR

Gl Zo TF/Ne Mn Kl

U. St. Auswärtiges Amt

Part I

Part I

BRITAIN'S ATTITUDE AFTER THE MUNICH AGREEMENT AND UP TO THE OCCUPATION OF BOHEMIA AND MORAVIA

[*Seven months passed between Mr Neville Chamberlain's final meeting with Adolf Hitler at Munich in September 1938, and the German Government's repudiation of the Anglo-German Naval Agreement in April 1939; in these seven months, relations between Britain and Germany suddenly and almost inexplicably worsened, so that what had seemed at the beginning like the dawning of a new era of peace, was recognised at its end to have been the prelude to an inevitable war. By the spring of 1939, a new system was being established against Germany, to replace the old one which had been dismantled at the time of Munich. The Munich Agreement, by which Britain, France and Italy agreed to the cession to Germany of the Sudeten territories of Czechoslovakia— territories vital to that country's defence—was hailed by Chamberlain's opponents like Anthony Eden, who had resigned his post as Foreign Secretary seven months before, as a 'bloodless victory won by Hitler'. And yet in the streets of Munich the crowds had reserved their cheers for the British Prime Minister, as the man whose actions had brought peace for their time. As Sir Arthur Bryant was to write to one of Hitler's closest friends and foreign affairs advisers a few weeks before war finally broke out, had there been an election immediately after Munich Mr Chamberlain would have been returned in triumph, for an enormous force of public opinion followed Chamberlain. Both countries' leaders signed a statement that 'we regard the Agreement signed last night, and the Anglo-German Naval Agreement, as symbolic of the desire of our two peoples never to go to war with one another again'. What was required more than anything else during this delicate period, in which the strained relations between both countries were to be healed and consolidated, was that there should be no violent disturbance to disrupt the sensitive meta- bolism of Anglo-German relations. Yet so forceful was the opposition among Parliamentarians to the Agreement, and so vociferous was the Press, that within only a few days of his return, Mr Chamberlain was declaring in the*

House of Commons that rearmament must go forward. Hitler retaliated in turn by a speech at Saarbrücken, in the course of which he prophesied that were Duff Cooper, Eden and Mr Churchill ever to come to power, Germany would know that their aim would be to launch a new world war. The three Englishmen named in the speech began to tour the country, spreading the sounds of alarm, and in this they were aided by one of those unplanned coincidences of history: a deranged Jew shot and killed a young German diplomat in Paris. Without waiting for sanction from his Führer, the German Propaganda Minister and others of his rank seized the opportunity to launch a country-wide assault on the Jews and Jewish property in Germany as revenge. This alone offended British public opinion quite enough, but when the German Press began to link the names of the most prominent anti-Germans in England with the murder of the diplomat, the British Government no longer felt able to ignore this change of tone in Anglo-German relations. Mr Chamberlain appealed to the Germans for a return to the spirit of Munich, but the alarm had been raised on both sides now, and the gap began to widen. Increasing and ill-founded anxiety was felt in the Foreign Office that Hitler might be considering an attack on the Western Powers, and they refused to believe the assurances of the British Ambassador in Berlin, Sir Nevile Henderson, during February that Hitler was not contemplating any adventures at that time. Encouraged in turn by the growing anti-German tendencies displayed in Britain, the Germans watched every sign that Britain was preparing to throw the Munich policy overboard.]

Chamberlain's Statements in Defence of his Munich Policy

With the signing of the Munich Agreement on 29 September 1938 and the subsequent Anglo-German Declaration[1] of the 30th, it seemed certain that Britain's relations with the Reich would be marked by a mutually acceptable settlement on the basis of friendly co-operation towards the peaceful solution of all the outstanding problems. Thus the British Prime Minister declared in a speech to the House of Commons on 3 October, 'I believe there are many who will feel with me that such a Declaration, signed by the German Chancellor and myself, is something more than a pious expression of opinion. In our relations with other countries, everything depends on there being sincerity and good will on both sides. I believe that there is sincerity and good will on both sides in this declaration. That is why to me its significance goes far beyond its actual words.' Elsewhere in his speech he said, 'After everything that has been said about the German Chancellor today and in the past I do feel that the House ought to recognise the difficulty for a man in that position to take back such emphatic declarations as he had already made and to recognise that consenting to discuss with representatives of other Powers those things which he had declared he had already decided once and for all, was a real and a substantial contribution on his part.'[2]

Henderson's Behaviour during the Discussions of the International Boundary Commission

During the work of the 'International Commission' on the settlement of the application of the Munich Agreement, an attitude of indecision was frequently shown by Britain's representative, the British Ambassador in Berlin, Sir Nevile Henderson; this meant that Britain was still intent on operating her own unrestricted policies in Europe. From the sources available to us, it is evident that during his attendance, Henderson repeatedly occasioned disputes in the conduct of the Commission's affairs by his behaviour.[3] In consequence, the only conclusion that could be drawn was that Britain was deliberately using her delegates to try to complicate the implementation of the Munich proposals.[4] That the British Prime Minister himself was concerned about this impression can be elicited from the message he sent through the British Embassy to the Führer on 5 October 1938 in view of the Führer's impending speech in the Sportpalast that day; in this message he expressed the hope that such differences could shortly be disposed of.[5]

Growing Opposition in Britain to the Munich Policy

The resignation of the First Lord of the Admiralty, Duff Cooper, on 1 October, was the first visible reaction of the opponents of the Munich Agreement. Although in Henderson's view this resignation in no way damaged the Prime Minister's position or prejudiced his policies (in a conversation with Attolico on 2 October 1938, Henderson exclaimed, 'I am very glad that he (Duff Cooper) has gone—he is a frightful fellow'[6]) it seemed to a certain extent a signal for a more critical examination to be made of the Government's policies by large sections of public opinion.[7] This criticism was seized upon by the Opposition and fanned by them. Daventry radio regarded Duff Cooper's resignation as proof of the 'doubts and apprehension' with which many circles viewed coming political events'.[8] This mood grew to such an extent during the

first days in October that Chamberlain saw himself obliged to request
the Führer, in the message referred to above, 'to go in closer detail in
some way into the contacts he had had with the Prime Minister, whereby he could give the Prime Minister some support in forming public
opinion in Britain', in his coming speech on 5 October.[9] On Chamberlain's internal political difficulties, a despatch from the Japanese Ambassador in London, Shigemitsu, dated 16 December, is also a significant
source. It states: 'There is mistrust of Chamberlain's policies in Britain,
and the atmosphere of opposition is consequently a strong one.'[10]

Exacerbation of Anglo-German Relations by our
Press Campaign of November 1938

A still further deterioration in this atmosphere resulted from the German
newspaper attacks on British politicians hostile to us after the murder
of Counsellor of Legation vom Rath in Paris; on 11 November 1938
the British Foreign Secretary Lord Halifax was constrained to direct his
Embassy in Berlin to protest to the Reich Government about these
attacks.[11] The British Foreign Secretary termed the publication of such
attacks indefensible, and in any case not in harmony with the spirit of
his conversations with them last November in Berlin, or with the intention of the Declaration signed by the Prime Minister and Reich Chancellor in Munich.[12] On 14 November 1938 the Prime Minister, Mr
Chamberlain, made a statement on this in the House of Commons.[13]
At the same time the anti-Jewish demonstrations in the Reich resulted in
an extremely violent British newpaper campaign against Germany, and
this lasted until the first major and official attack on the 'Munich' policy
was launched in the House of Commons, on 19 December, with the
Prime Minister being forced to defend his policy on a Vote of Confidence by the Socialists. The statement in his speech to the effect that he
was still waiting for some sign from the Reich Government that it was
ready to make its contribution to peace, was construed by the British
public as the first sign of a wavering in Chamberlain's confidence in
German behaviour after the Munich talks.[14] The *Manchester Guardian* of
20 December 1938 significantly headed its leading article devoted to
Chamberlain's statement 'The Awakening?'. The consequence of this
development, and of the rearmament measures being supported by the
British Government, was, as the Japanese Ambassador in London,
Shigemitsu, described in his despatch on 16 December, that there was

a prevalent mood in Britain that they were opposed to any German hegemony being established on the Continent, and this would be smashed when the time came and they themselves were strong enough;[15] these opinions were growing increasingly powerful even amongst the Conservatives' supporters.[16]

Shigemitsu added that there was nobody who was against rearmament, and that it was being put into effect with all possible despatch.

Signs of a Move towards Disengagement from the Munich Policy at the Outset of 1939

Certain occurrences in the first months of 1939 indicated that British policy was already beginning to diverge from the course agreed at Munich: these included the continued Anglo-French collaboration, which was officially admitted by the French Foreign Minister Bonnet on 26 January 1939, and by Prime Minister Chamberlain on 6 February 1939;[17] Hudson's trip to Warsaw and Moscow[18] and the attendance of Halifax and Churchill at the banquet arranged at the Russian Embassy in London, after very delicate negotiations between the Russian Ambassador Maisky and the Foreign Office.[19]

Renunciation of Munich as a Reaction to the German Occupation of Bohemia and Moravia

The events in what had been Czechoslovakia and the German entry into Bohemia and Moravia on 15 March 1939 then determined the final course of British foreign policy. Although Chamberlain announced in the House of Commons on 14 March 1939,[20] apropos of the British guarantee to Czechoslovakia, that the situation remained unchanged, as the guarantee had referred only to an unprovoked aggression—which had not however taken place—and although on 14 March 1939 he also informed the Reich Government through his Embassy in Berlin that the British Government 'have no desire to interfere unnecessarily in matters with which other Governments may be more directly concerned' than Britain,[21] yet at the same time and in the same communication the Prime Minister warned that the British Government was very concerned for the success of all the efforts that had been made to restore confidence and relax tension in Europe; and he declared even more clearly in his House of Commons speech on 23 March that Germany would meet determined opposition from Britain and other countries, if she was aiming to go even further after this.[22] Even harsher was the tone of his speech at Birmingham on 17 March, in which he said that the German people would live bitterly to regret the step they had just taken.[23] The Bulgarian Minister in London, Momtchiloff, reported in an 'official commentary' on this Birmingham speech that it marked the Prime Minister's abandonment of his Munich policies.[24] Halifax's remark in the House of Lords on 20 March that the Munich Agreement was a 'tragic error in British foreign policy' confirms this report by Momtchiloff.[25]

In its Note to the German Government, the British Government endeavoured to throw the blame for the breakdown of the Munich Agreement on to Germany. In this message, which the British Embassy in Berlin was (on 17 March) instructed to hand to the German Government, it was stated that the British Government desired to make it plain that while they intended to take no action themselves, they could not but regard the events of the past few days as a complete repudiation of the Munich Agreement and a denial of the spirit in which the negotiators of that Agreement had bound themselves. At the same time the British Government protested at the changes affected in Czecho-Slovakia [*hyphenated now* !] by German military action, which in the British Government's view were devoid of any basis of legality.[26]

On 19 March the British Ambassador, Sir Nevile Henderson, travelled to London to report.[27] On the same day the German Ambassador, von Dirksen, left London and returned to Berlin.[28]

Part II

Part II

THE BRITISH POLICY OF ENCIRCLEMENT

[*In the section of the German report which follows, the* Forschungsamt *organised its material in a manner which might confuse the issue—attending to each Balkan country's relations with Britain in turn, when in fact the developing crisis needs to be viewed chronologically. The German occupation of the rest of Czecho-Slovakia in mid-March 1939 marked the end of the Munich period for the British. The British Ambassador's recall from Berlin on 17 March was intended as a token of Britain's displeasure, and Mr Chamberlain spoke in strong terms of his fears that this German move into Czecho-Slovakia was to be followed by other attacks on small states. All the greater was the alarm which was therefore felt when the Rumanian Minister in London, M. Tilea, reported to the Foreign Secretary Lord Halifax the alarming but unfounded news that his country was in danger of invasion by German troops—an echo which was to set off an avalanche. Believing this report all-too uncritically, the British Prime Minister drafted a declaration of collective security which the French, Soviet and Polish Governments were invited to sign. A guarantee was offered to Rumania, although there was no possible manner in which Britain could have gone to her assistance. As Hitler advised the Rumanian Foreign Minister on 19 April, the guarantee could never be realised; and von Ribbentrop advised M. Gafencu further that it would 'make a bad impression' in Berlin if Rumania were to participate in the British policy of 'encirclement' against Germany. Each new British and French move was now viewed in the light of this threat of encirclement—a word fraught with almost Freudian connotations for the Germans, recalling all the indignities and deprivations they had suffered during the Great War. When the Hungarian Prime Minister Count Teleki visited Berlin at the end of April, he was also warned by Hitler and von Ribbentrop to take no part in the encirclement of Germany. Initially, the Rumanian, Hungarian and Yugoslav Governments all indicated to the Germans their readiness to ignore the British overtures. Not so the Poles: similar rumours of German troop movements towards the Polish frontiers had been followed by a similar unilateral guarantee from Britain to Poland on 30 March, announced in the*

*House of Commons next day by the Prime Minister; within a week the Polish
Foreign Minister Colonel Beck had visited London of his own volition, and an
Anglo-Polish Treaty of Alliance had been signed (but not ratified), a considerable reversal of Polish foreign policy up to that point. The final blow to peace
in the Balkans was struck on 7 April when, without any warning to Germany,
Italy invaded Albania: now Britain met greater encouragement, and concluded
treaties of mutual assistance with Greece and Rumania on 13 April, and then
a month later concluded negotiations with Turkey on a hasty and provisional
alliance which was, however, destined never to operate. It was towards Turkey
in particular that Germany turned her most anxious gaze during the months that
followed, for although Rumania and the other countries had still refused to
participate in the 'encirclement' of Germany, it was still an open question
whether Turkey would become involved in this policy. Von Ribbentrop
called Baron Franz von Papen to him immediately after the Italian invasion of
Albania, and told him he was sending him to Ankara as German Ambassador;
he told von Papen that if the ring of 'encirclement' were closed, as had almost
been the case in 1914, this time with the participation of Turkey, there would
be no alternative to war—a war which would probably be lost. Turkey was less
afraid of Germany than of Italy, whose plans for a new Roman Empire had
been well announced, and who already possessed a fringe of islands within
Turkish territorial waters; but during the months that preceded the outbreak of
war, the Germans could read into the intercepted reports of Turkish diplomats
every indication that Turkey was in fact endeavouring to promote a British
policy of encirclement, and even to draw the Soviet Union in.]*

The Encirclement Programme and the First
Diplomatic Steps towards its Fulfilment

The repudiation of the German-Czech Agreement of 15 March, and
Henderson's recall to London were regarded primarily as a grave warning to Germany, according to a despatch by the Yugoslav Counsellor
Dragutinovic in Geneva. However, the western Powers desired to avoid
open conflict at that time, according to this source, and by taking suitable
diplomatic steps among the lesser Powers (Poland, Rumania, Yugoslavia, Belgium and Holland) and the Soviet Union they planned to win
time to prepare for resistance in the future. The Bulgarian Minister in
London, Momtchiloff, made a similar comment on 16 March: according to confidential information in his possession, he said, the true intention of the British Government was to play for time and to undertake

nothing final until they were ready to intervene in strength.[1] Two days later, Momtchiloff reported that energetic diplomatic activity by the British was imminent in the Balkans.[2] With French Government support the British Government did indeed take the initiative—as was confirmed to the Yugoslav Minister in Paris by the Quai d'Orsay[3]—in inquiring of those powers 'exposed to a threat from the Reich' whether they were prepared to undertake concerted action with the object of preventing any further German expansion, and they [the British] began a series of active diplomatic discussions along these lines with the interested Powers on 18 March.

In answer to a Question in the House of Commons on 28 March, Mr Chamberlain was obliged to admit that these conversations with other Governments went a great deal further than consultations.[4]

British Plans in the Balkans

As far as the shape of the British plans in the Balkans were concerned, Momtchiloff stated on 17 April that the British diplomatic activity was aimed at improving their mutual solidarity and establishing more intimate collaboration between the Balkan states in providing security as a unified bloc.[5] Britain expected that such a bloc would primarily adopt the stance of a neutral power, and this would hamper the possible German and Italian attempts at expansion into the Balkans, and provide for a joint defence of the Balkan frontiers in the event of war. Momtchiloff added to this that the Foreign Office had given him this information while 'dropping a broad hint' that Britain was becoming increasingly convinced of the possibility of such a German and Italian aggression on the Balkans.

As early as 5 April Momtchiloff had told his Foreign Ministry that the Foreign Office considered it essential that the Balkan Pact be linked to the Agreement with Poland, and steps had been undertaken to achieve this with a minimum of delay.[6] As Momtchiloff claimed to have learned 'from Turkish and Yugoslav sources', the Foreign Office had assured itself of the support of Paris and Ankara in putting these plans into effect.[7]

The tactics adopted by Britain to put into effect her plans for encirclement did not escape some criticism. The Permanent Under-Secretary in the Greek Foreign Ministry, Mavroudis, said that he thought the manner in which Britain had carried out her ideas on encirclement left much to be desired, to say the least. He knew for a fact that this had caused some harm. The consultations should have been carried out with greatest caution and with utmost secrecy, but by all appearances Britain had been concerned only to make a good impression on her own public opinion.[8]

The Anglo-Turkish Treaty Negotiations:

The Conflict of Anglo-Italian Interests; Influence of the Italian Occupation of Albania on Turkey's Readiness to Sign the Treaty; The First British Proposal and the Turkish Reply; Turkish Interest in Co-operation with the U.S.S.R.; Difficulties over 'Article 6' of the Draft Treaty.

For the objectives sought after by Britain in Turkey, a remark by the British Deputy Secretary General at the League of Nations, F. P. Walters is very revealing.[9] According to Walters, Britain attached the highest importance to Turkey in the formation of a defensive coalition in the South-East, as in the event of a conflict the presence of Turkey in such a defensive alliance would enable the Western Powers to maintain intact their lines of communication to the East, through Turkey; moreover, the Turkish Straits [the Dardanelles] would not be the major obstacle they had been in the last war.[10] Italy would probably have to be regarded as something of an obstacle to this line of communication, said Walters further, but that was of less moment than the obstacle presented by the Turkish Straits. An opinion from Italian sources confirms very clearly the fact that in her wooing of the Turks Britain must inevitably come into conflict with Italian interests. For example the Italian Ambassador in Ankara, de Peppo, said in December 1938: 'The predominant influence of Britain in Turkey has always prevented the development of any trusting relationship between Turkey and Italy. All Italy's exertions to persuade Turkey that Italy has no aggressive designs on her, have had negative results.'[11]

Italy's occupation of Albania, which began on 7 April 1939, must have been of decisive importance in determining Turkey's attitude to the British overtures to her. As the Turkish Ambassador in London, Rüstü Aras, stated, the Turkish Government held the view that the occupation of Albania was a hostile act against the Balkan States, and conjured up the immediate danger of further aggression by Italy in the Balkans.[12]

This situation was at once exploited by Britain to show to Turkey the first draft of a Mutual Assistance Pact; in this initially only a possible conflict with Italy was taken into account, but subsequently reference was also made to a 'German threat' in a proposed addition. A brief sent by the Turkish Foreign Minister to the Turkish Embassy in Moscow on 27 April refers to this in the following terms:[13]

'At the end of this week the British Ambassador (*Forschungsamt:* 'Sir Hughe Knatchbull-Hugessen') brought me a proposal from his Government. This proposal states: "In the event that Turkey should offer armed resistance to a threat to her freedom in the Mediterranean or to any other direct or indirect threat from Italy, the British Government will be ready on principle to go to Turkey's assistance, on condition that if Britain should be drawn into a war with Italy, Turkey should also be prepared to help the British Government. In order that the situations in which the above mutual commitments should come into force may be explicitly defined, it will be necessary to set up certain basic principles." Since making this proposal, the British have expanded their suggestions to embrace a potential threat from Germany as well.'

On 16 April 1939 the Foreign Ministry in Ankara transmitted to the Turkish Ambassador in London the following reply to these British proposals:[14]

'The domination of Europe by the Axis Powers and the endangering of the existence of the small countries constitute eventualities totally opposed to the interests of general peace and of their national affairs, particularly in the case of Turkey, even if she herself is not the object of any direct threats or aggression. The possibility of an Italian domination of the Mediterranean poses as clear a threat to Turkey as to Britain.

'This throws into sharp relief the close [correspondence] existing between Turkey's interests and those of Great Britain at the present conjuncture . . .*

* [The German document omits one paragraph here, reading: 'The Ministry of Foreign Affairs believes it necessary to expound the following considerations in order to establish beyond possible doubt the line the Turkish Government proposes to follow in practice, in face of such a situation as defined above.' The following paragraph is so mutilated in the German document, owing to the inability of the deciphering personnel to break the code down completely, that this translation, prepared with the aid of the original French communication, does not reflect the incoherence of the original German text. See illustration on page 14.]

'This allows the close . . . (*Forschungsamt:* 'indecipherable') of the . . . * Turkish and British interests in the present situation to appear quite clearly. In fact, Turkey faced with this position is . . .*, in that the course of conduct which she will follow is quite public, and in that Turkey in the matter of the choice before her is compelled to give due weight to these considerations (and?) it is already clear, in the event that the Axis should take up its position against her—if the Mediterranean states should want . . .* a new world war, then they will show this with all force in a very short time at the Dardanelles, then Turkey will be compelled to oppose the pressure of the Axis, so that in this situation it needs no explanation that where possible France and the Soviet Union . . . * being—on the . . . * support with assistance, and that in the face of this necessity . . .* to know and to decide, to be able to make a decision –it is to a certain extent important for us to . . .* the way in which the Soviet Union will act. In our previous enquiries, we have not yet . . . *. The defence . . . *, which falls to our lot at the Dardanelles is so important that the despatch of our forces beyond our frontiers to the assistance of Rumania neither is possible, nor would correspond to the general or common interest. The fact that we are committed against the Axis will increase the importance and the bargaining power of Bulgaria. Therefore we believe that the efforts to maintain the solidarity of the Balkan States and to . . . * the Balkan States against the irruption of Axis influence, and what we have so far done, is the greatest effort that Turkey can make which can serve the general interests of peace.

'For today we can summarize these . . .* as follows:

1. No one should be kept in doubt that, in accordance with the course of events . . . *, we shall go with Britain in support of the general interests of peace, or will follow . . . * a policy, and that we shall remain neutral as long as the Axis powers do not go over to the attack in the Balkans or the Mediterranean.

2. Great . . . * must support the defensive preparations we have undertaken to defend our territories in case of necessity against the Axis powers.

3. All efforts must be made to secure the co-operation of the Soviet Union.

* *Forschungsamt:* 'indecipherable'.

4. Britain must provide her support so as to . . . * a step between Rumania and Bulgaria.

5. In order that, if the *casus foederis* arises, we can act together, we must now be informed on the project mentioned in your note.

6. The points mentioned above and . . .* must remain completely secret.'

It is evident from this Turkish reply that Turkey was strongly concerned to secure Russian co-operation in the encirclement operation.[15]

When it was announced in London on 12 May 1939[16] that the British and Turkish Governments were committing themselves, even before the final Treaty was signed[17] to effective co-operation and mutual assistance in the event that war broke out in the Mediterranean, it caused some concern among the Turks that the Russians reacted with extreme reserve to this Anglo-Turkish Declaration. According to a despatch from the Turkish Ambassador in Moscow, Apaydin, on 13 May, he had expressed his astonishment to the [Soviet] Foreign Ministry that neither the Russian radio nor the Russian newspapers had published so much as one word about the Anglo-Turkish Declaration.[18] In his despatch, Apaydin commented further that wrong conclusions might be drawn from this Russian attitude, and he was requesting an interview with the Deputy Foreign Minister Potemkin about it. On the following day, the Ambassador reported that while the newspapers had now published a digest of the Declaration, received from the Tass agency in Ankara, they had refrained from making any comment on it.

Since Turkey was endeavouring to pay the closest attention to Russia's attitude, even during her subsequent Treaty negotiations with the British, she was very disappointed, as the Japanese Ambassador in Ankara, Taketomi reported on 7 July, that the parallel talks between Britain and Russia were making such slow and unsuccessful headway.[19]

Although both by its wording and by the manner and circumstance of its publication the Anglo-Turkish Declaration of 12 May 1939 was primarily of a demonstrative character, the Yugoslav chargé d'affaires in London, Tomazeo, nevertheless concluded, from the fact that Britain—as he reported—began to supply Turkey 'at accelerated rate' at the end of May with 'vast amounts' of war supplies, that the impending Anglo-Turkish Treaty of Alliance was pursuing quite concrete aims and was not just a means of applying pressure.[20]

A despatch from the Yugoslav Legation in Ankara dated 1 July 1939

* *Forschungsamt:* 'indecipherable'.

deals with the particular difficulties emerging during the Anglo-Turkish Treaty negotiations in consequence of the controversial Article Six of the Anglo-Turkish Declaration of 12 May 1939:[21] according to this source, 'they' did not dare to include the point concerning the safety of the Balkans in the Draft Treaty; but, the despatch continues, it was planned to mention Rumania and Greece by including in the Treaty's text a passage whereby Turkey would join Britain in the event of an attack on one of these countries and the consequent coming into force of the British guarantee.[22]

Rumania's Role in the Encirclement

First Reports of Britain's Intention of Giving Rumania a Guarantee as well. The British Guarantee Announced. Gafencu's Visit to London.

On 17 March, the Rumanian Minister in London, M. Tilea, was directed by his Government to call on Lord Halifax, as the Yugoslav chargé d'affaires in London Milanovic reported, to tell him of Germany's 'economic ultimatum' and to ask the British Government for aid.[23] Milanovic continued that Tilea had told him that the Rumanian Government was exploiting the incident (i.e. these German demands) to increase tension and to safeguard Rumania's security in every possible contingency; he (Tilea) had accordingly 'made the utmost possible use of his instructions'. Halifax, reported Milanovic in conclusion, had replied to the Rumanian appeal that Rumania could in principle count on Britain's support.

Early in April, the Yugoslav Legation in London reported to Belgrade that while during the Anglo-Polish talks they had decided to do without Rumanian participation in the Anglo-Polish Treaty, Britain and France would issue a similar Declaration in respect of Rumania as they had for Poland.[24]

When first reports appeared in the British and French press about an extension of the British guarantee to include Rumania as well, they were not reproduced in the Rumanian press, according to a report of the Italian Minister in Bucharest, Chigi, dated 9 April 1939.[25] Chigi commented that as late as 3 April the Rumanian government had still had no official knowledge whatsoever of an imminent British guarantee, and they had expressly declared that they had taken no such initiative themselves, nor did they want to.

On 13 April, the British guarantees for Rumania and Greece were announced in the House of Commons by the Prime Minister:

'His Majesty's Government feel that they have both a duty and a service to perform by leaving no doubt in the mind of anyone as to their own position. I therefore take this opportunity of saying that His Majesty's Government attach the greatest importance to the avoidance of disturbance of the *status quo* in the Mediterranean and the Balkan Peninsular. Consequently, they have come to the conclusion that in the event of any action being taken which [clearly] threatened the independence of Greece or Rumania and which the Greek or Rumanian Governments respectively considered it vital to resist with their national forces, His Majesty's Government would feel themselves bound at once to lend the Greek or Rumanian Governments all the support in their power. We are communicating this declaration to the Governments directly concerned and to others, especially Turkey.'[26]

Before the Rumanian Foreign Minister Gafencu set out on his journey to Berlin, London and Paris, various guidelines were discussed and decided in the Rumanian State Council for the foreign policy Gafencu was to represent in the European capitals, according to what the Rumanian ambassador in Paris, Tatarescu, told the Yugoslav Minister Puric; these guidelines had as their purport that Rumania wanted to establish good relations with all the Great Powers, without favouring any one of them above the others.[27] The Anglo-French Guarantee to her placed no obligations on Rumania, and Rumania would equally accept similar guarantees from Germany, Italy or Russia if these were offered. But in view of her economic ties with Germany, Rumania, while reserving her independence, would afford her her utmost cooperation. As she needed certain imports and credits for her rearmament programme, Rumania would follow the appropriate policies with Britain and France.

Gafencu was in London from 23 to 26 April.[28] The reports of his discussions and their outcome are to some extent conflicting, but one thing is certain, that Gafencu asked for British credits and was given them.[29] Gafencu himself told the Rumanian Prime Minister Calinescu on 24 April that while his talks were still in progress, he could already state that he was satisfied in any case, and he had not been in opposition for one moment.[30] Many suggestions had been made to him, which he had received with the reserve dictated by Rumania's situation. In general his reception in London had been 'quite extraordinary'. On the other hand the Yugoslav Foreign Ministry was informed via Paris on 25 April that Gafencu had declared in London that Rumania was not in a position to enter into any organisation aligned against Germany, and particularly not together with Russia.[31] To the British he was said to have quoted Hitler's words: 'Britain is offering guarantees in the shape of the French Army. There is no doubt that this is one of the finest in the world, but it cannot defend the whole world, and least of all Rumania.'[32] Altogether—according to this despatch from Paris—Gafencu's visit to London was regarded as a failure of Chamberlain's policies; it had left behind an unexpectedly unfavourable impression.[33]

Shigemitsu, the Japanese Ambassador in London, also reported on 30 May 1939 that there was growing dissatisfaction in Britain over Rumania's attitude.[34] Rumania appeared to be trying to adopt the same neutral attitude as Belgium, even though the prosecution of such a policy would encounter grave difficulties on account of the quite different circumstances—particularly since Rumania had already fallen under the German sway in consequence of her economic agreement and her dependence on munitions deliveries from the [German-controlled] Skoda Works. Expert opinion therefore was that from the military point of view Rumania would be nothing but a burden for the Western Powers, and that for this reason the best the *Entente* countries could hope for was her continued neutrality.

In the period following the announcement of the British Guarantee, some effort was invested on the extension of the guarantees already given to Greece and Rumania, and on the definition of how Turkey, Greece and Rumania should collaborate within the framework of a comprehensive guarantee system, according to a despatch by the Yugoslav Minister in Ankara, Sumenkovic. As far as Greece was concerned, Sumenkovic added, some progress had been made, but not so with Rumania as her position was different in both fact and law.[35]

Britain Announces her Guarantee to Greece

On 13 April the British guarantee to Greece was announced simultaneously with that to Rumania.[36] The Foreign Ministry in Warsaw had expected such a British Guarantee to be given to Greece as early as 11 April, and had assumed that immediately after Chamberlain's declaration to that effect had been published, British troops would land on Corfu and Crete to forestall the Italians.[37]

When once before, reports had appeared in newspapers that Britain was on the point of offering a guarantee to Greece, the Under-Secretary of State in the Greek Foreign Ministry, M. Mavroudis, had commented to the Yugoslav Minister in Athens on 9 April that the British Minister there had so far made nothing of this known to the Greek Government.[38] The press reports concerned, which he was not inclined to believe, could only do damage to Greece and Rumania in their situation *vis-à-vis* Italy and Germany. In the event that Britain desired of her own volition to protect Greece, Mavroudis had added, Greece would not insist on restraining Britain; but to third parties she would adopt the attitude that Greece would be happy to accept similar offers from any other quarter. With regard to the British conversations, Mavroudis further stated that while Greece would make what would amount to a favourable reply she was in no position to do this in public, but would be obliged to reply that in view of her own position it mattered not a little to her to discuss such questions fully in advance.[39] That Mavroudis was a strong critic of the methods used by the British in consultation has been referred to already (on page 57 above).

Like Mavroudis, the Greek Minister in London commented that Greece had asked for neither a guarantee nor a pact from Britain, nor would she be making any proposals of that nature. In reporting this comment on 12 April, the Yugoslav Minister in London concluded by saying that Britain and France would probably furnish only a unilateral guarantee, but would prepare a secret plan for military cooperation in an emergency.[40]

Shigemitsu, the Japanese Ambassador in London, discoursed at length in a report of 30 May, on the subject of Greece's attitude now that the British and French guarantee had been given.[41] He inclined toward the view that Greece would maintain a benevolent neutrality towards the guarantor countries, Britain, France and Turkey.

The British Woo Bulgaria

**Plans for the Inclusion of Bulgaria in a
Comprehensive Balkan System.
Probing the Bulgarian Conditions.
British Approaches to Rumania and Greece over
Concession to be Granted to Bulgaria by these Countries.**

That Britain was also implicating Bulgaria in her diplomatic activities in the Balkans first became clear from a despatch from the Bulgarian Minister in London, Momtchiloff, on 15 April 1939, in which he states that British plans in the Balkans were being continued even after the guarantee to Rumania, with concessions to be made to Bulgaria in which the British would be supported, as Turkish and Yugoslav sources claimed, by Paris and Ankara.[42] On 17 April a 'broad hint' had been dropped in the Foreign Office to the Bulgarian Minister Momtchiloff[43] —as he related to the Yugoslav chargé d'affaires in London—that Britain was becoming increasingly persuaded of the possibility of an Axis attack on the Balkans, and that her diplomatic activity was accordingly aimed at supporting collective security and creating more intimate cooperation among the Balkan countries to promote their security as a unified bloc; Britain would primarily expect from this bloc that it declared itself a large neutral force, and that it would defend the Balkan frontiers collectively in the event of war. This would forestall any German or Italian venture attempted in the Balkans. As Momtchiloff further related to Milanovic, the British Foreign Secretary, Lord Halifax, had enquired extensively of him as to Bulgaria's attitude and the possibility of cooperation among the Balkan countries; he, Momtchiloff, had replied that Bulgaria was moved by a desire to maintain good relations with the Balkan states and not to be accomplice to any extremist venture put up by Germany or Italy, for as he (Momtchiloff) had added all intelligent Bulgarians knew that it would be a catastrophe for Bulgaria to tie herself to a power bloc which was then beaten in war. To the Yugoslav chargé d'affaires Momtchiloff expressed the belief that the British Government would transfer the burden of its negotiations to Sofia as he himself [as Minister in London] had received no concrete suggestions or proposals from the Foreign Office.[44]

Immediately after Italy's annexation of Albania the British Minister in Sofia had indeed asked the Bulgarian Prime Minister Kiosseivanoff under what circumstances Bulgaria would be prepared for a *rapprochement* and cooperation with Greece, to which Kiosseivanoff had replied that this would be possible only and solely on condition that Greece relinquished certain territories to her.[45] As the Yugoslav Minister in Sofia learned soon after from Kiosseivanoff, Britain continued to probe discreetly in Sofia as to whether if Bulgaria received southern Dobruja from Rumania she would agree to sign a collective security pact with Rumania. According to the version he gave the Yugoslav Minister [in Berlin] Kiosseivanoff replied to the British hint in the vein that Bulgaria did not desire to defend Rumania's frontiers at the Carpathians or indeed anywhere else.[46]

There are many reports available which indicate that Britain took some pains in Bucharest to try to resolve the differences between these two countries by means of Rumanian concessions to the Bulgarian demands.[47] The reconciliation of Rumania with Bulgaria is also said to have been a topic of Gafencu's visits to London and Paris; the Rumanian Foreign Minister is said to have declared that he would make this the subject of a report to King Carol.[48]

While it therefore seems that Rumania was at all events not averse to the concessions the British suggested she make to Bulgaria, Greece— evidently even before any concrete *démarche* had been undertaken by the British in Athens—informed London that she would oppose most strenuously any suggestion of territorial concessions to Bulgaria; this becomes evident from a report of the Yugoslav Minister in Athens, on a conversation with the Under-Secretary of State in the Greek Foreign Ministry, Mavroudis, on 20 April.[49]

As a gap had thus emerged between the Bulgarian demands and the Greek attitude to them, the British plans in Bulgaria evidently broke down at this preparatory stage;[50] for in May 1939 the Bulgarian Minister in London, Momtchiloff, stated that so far Britain had made no concrete proposals to Bulgaria, either through him or in Sofia, and that there was no prospect of any territorial concessions in the Dobruja.[51] Further evidence that Britain's wooing of Bulgaria had yielded no tangible results can be seen in the fact that Kiosseivanoff ordered the journey of the President of the Chamber of Deputies, Mashanoff, to London to be postponed, and when Mashanoff still went ahead with his trip to London in July 1939 without his consent, he tried to strip it of any political importance. Kiosseivanoff expressly forbade the Bulgarian Minister in London to attend any banquets or dinners given in honour of Masha-noff,[52] and told the Yugoslav Minister in Sofia that the visit by Masha-noff—who had entrusted himself with some kind of mission—had been exploited by London and Paris to undermine the importance of his (Kiosseivanoff's) visit to Berlin.[53] Then again, in August 1939 Momt-chiloff was to report to the Foreign Ministry in Sofia that a new attempt at agreement on the Dobruja question might be undertaken, and that in the British Foreign Office there seemed some prospect of a solution to the problem.[54] He asked for instructions, if thought opportune, on whether he should undertake a *démarche* along these lines.

British Policy Towards Yugoslavia

British Hopes in Yugoslavia before
Stoyadinovic's Resignation;
The Visit by Prince-Regent Paul in London.

If in Bulgaria Britain's attempts to draw Sofia into an encirclement front
had met hitherto insurmountable difficulties in the shape of the local
foreign policy's association with territorial demands, in Yugoslavia
British diplomacy was to come to grief on Belgrade's ties to Rome.
London continued to fasten some hope on the former Prime and Foreign
Minister, Stoyadinovic, to whose journey to London in October 1937
a number of expectations had been coupled. Certain of Stoyadinovic's
statements in London,[55] together with the Yugoslav attitude at Nyons,[56]
the extension of the Franco-Yugoslav treaty of friendship for a further
five years and not least in importance the Foreign Minister's active
business links with Britain, which played a not insignificant part in
Anglo-Yugoslav relations in the view of the *Observer*'s Vienna correspondent Fodor, encouraged the hope that in the event of a serious
conflict Yugoslavia would in the final analysis come down on the side
of her old ally, according to Fodor.[57] The journey of Prince-Regent Paul
and Princess Olga to London in November 1938 was also designed to
promote more intimate relations between Yugoslavia and Britain, as
the Head of the Press Office, Lukovic, explained.

Stoyadinovic's resignation early in February 1939 and Italy's occupation of Albania in April of that year focused renewed attention on
[Yugoslavia's] policy towards Italy and one of the results of the Prince
Regent's visit to Berlin from 1 to 8 June was to cause the British Press
to speak in terms of German and Italian pressure on Yugoslavia. The
further visit paid by the Prince Regent and his wife to London in July
1939 led to speculation in London diplomatic circles, according to a
report from the Yugoslav Minister in Sofia, Jurisic, on 13 July, that the
Prince Regent had wanted to assure the British Government that
Yugoslavia had not joined the Axis camp and was maintaining her
independent policies.[58] At the same time there was talk in newspaper
circles that this visit to London and the trip by the Finance Minister to
the South of France and to Britain in July were intended as a counter to
the German pressure, and the Bulgarian Minister in London, Momtchiloff, reported on 2 August 1939 that after the Prince-Regent's visit
London now had more confidence in Yugoslavia's friendship.[59]

There are available only a few diplomatic despatches which throw light on the topics and results of these talks in London. Thus the Japanese Consul-General in Vienna, Yamji, informed the Foreign Ministry in Tokyo on 3 August that according to one agent's report Britain had demanded of Yugoslavia that she *inter alia* prevent Bulgaria from taking any rash steps.[60] Further, Britain was said to have expressed the desire that Yugoslavia make military preparations on her frontier with Albania (despite the neutrality she would need in any emergency in view of her geographical position) and later join an Anglo-Franco-Greek alliance, for which after the war she would get the ports of Zara, Fiume, Trieste and Pola. The Bulgarian Minister in London, Momtchiloff, informed his Foreign Ministry in Sofia on 2 August 1939 that Britain now hoped that Yugoslavia would prevent the Axis from exploiting the Balkans as a base for their operations.[61] In addition to this, the Prince Regent had expressed willingness to talk about credits. These versions are disputed in the report transmitted by the Yugoslav Foreign Minister Cincar-Markovic to the Yugoslav Legation in Berlin on 13 August;[62] in this it is said that during the visit to London there had neither been talk of a political agreement nor had anything of that nature been demanded by the British. Likewise, the Yugoslav Minister in London, Subotic, declared to the German ambassador, as he told his Foreign Ministry, that the Prince Regent's visit to London would not alter Yugoslavia's foreign policies.[63]

The Anglo-Soviet Negotiations

As the news agency Tass announced on 21 March, the British Government, alarmed by rumours of a German ultimatum to Rumania which had been put about by the Rumanian Minister in London, M. Tilea, on the occasion of the German-Rumanian economic conversations during March 1939 (see page 62 above), asked the Soviet Government on 18 March[64] what its attitude would be in the event of a German aggression against Rumania. The months of Anglo-Soviet discussions touched off by this cannot be completely followed from those sources now available —at least not as far as their precise course and the separate phases are concerned.[65] If one is to anticipate the conclusions of an overall analysis of the diplomatic despatches in question familiar to the *Forschungsamt*, it can be stated that the negotiating parties held widely divergent views, that Russia repeatedly complicated the basis of the discussions by advancing new requirements, while Britain for her part sought formulæ to

overcome the substantial obstacles thus created; and that finally there
was a growing tendency for both sides more or less to drag the talks
out in the hope that through some change in the general situation, or
through the occurrence of unexpected events, the negotiating partners
might become less intransigent or their own interests would permit a
less ambiguous stand to be made—in other words that one side's misgivings about the other side's demands would eventually subside.

The British Proposals and the Russian Counter-Proposals and Conditions

The following picture emerges of the British proposals and the Russian
counter-proposals. Initially Britain demanded from the Soviet Union
her assistance for Poland and Rumania;[66] but the Russians for their part
argued, according to what the Soviet chargé d'affaires in London told
the Yugoslav chargé d'affaires Milanovic, that peace was indivisible,
and they therefore proposed the summoning of a conference on keeping
the peace in the Far East as well.[67] When this was not accepted by the
British, they made a further proposal that they and Britain conclude a
mutual assistance pact making no reference to the Far East.[68] On the
scale of the alliances suggested by Moscow, the reports differ: while for
example the Soviet chargé d'affaires in London (according to Milanovic's despatch[69]) declared that the Soviet Union was agreeable to an
Alliance directed virtually against Germany alone, Molotov declared
(according to a despatch from the Turkish Ambassador in Moscow,
Apaydin) that he wanted the Pact to be aligned against an attack not only
from Germany but from any quarter, and that he wanted the three
countries (*Forschungsamt:* 'i.e. Russia, Britain and France') to give a joint
guarantee to the Soviet Union's border neighbours. Molotov took the
opportunity of pointing out that Britain had after all already entered
into mutual aid pacts with Turkey and Poland.[70] From a version of the
Soviet counter-proposals furnished by the Soviet Ambassador in
Ankara, Terentyev, the Soviet Union was demanding a tripartite
guarantee embracing all three countries (*Forschungsamt:* 'i.e. Russia,
Britain and France') in which all the Soviet Union's (*Forschungsamt:*
'European') neighbours were to be included.[71]

Britain on the other hand did not, according to a despatch from the
Yugoslav chargé d'affaires Milanovic in London, want to embark on a
full-scale alliance with Russia and tried to meet Russia's wishes by

modifying her original proposals.[72] According to the despatch already mentioned, she proposed that Russia should announce that in the event of an act of aggression she would intervene; in this case there would be no need to specify which other countries would do the intervening because some of these did not want to be mentioned. To give to Russia the safeguard she would want against finding herself fighting Germany alone as a consequence of this guarantee, this proposal also provided that the Russians should only intervene in cases where Britain and France were already at war for the same reason. As even this British proposal did not satisfy the Soviet Government, Britain finally resolved to propose that the countries to be guaranteed should be listed in a secret protocol, and to advocate that Soviet-Turkish and Soviet-Polish Agreements should be concluded.[73]

From these proposals and counter-proposals alone there emerges clearly the great extent to which the basis of the discussion was complicated by the Soviet Union's insistence on the inclusion of all her neighbouring countries in the joint guarantee commitment, for Lord Halifax was adamant that the independence of the Baltic states should be respected.[74] The difficulties became even more formidable when Russia expanded her demands in respect of the guarantee to her neighbours, so that even an 'indirect aggression'—i.e. a change of Government in one of these countries caused by the peaceful intervention of a third— was to be regarded as a *casus belli* in the sense of the guarantee commitment.[75] Another complication which the Soviet Russians dragged into the talks was, according to a despatch of the Bulgarian Minister in London, Momtchiloff, on 5 April, the Russian refusal to allow British warships to pass through the Dardanelles to go to Rumania's assistance.[76] It also emerges from Apaydin's despatches on 21 April and 24 May that the Soviet Union attached great importance to this matter of the defence of the Straits.[77]

Under the circumstances it is hardly surprising that all the despatches that touched upon the progress and course of the Anglo-Soviet talks were unanimously pessimistic as to the eventual outcome: Vansittart told the Yugoslav Minister in London that the talks were making little headway—as soon as one problem had been resolved, the Soviets brought up a new one.[78] On 19 July the U.S. Ambassador in Warsaw, Mr Drexel Biddle, commented that Strang had run aground.[79] The Japanese Minister in Stockholm reported that Strang had not been made particularly welcome by Moscow—on his arrival new demands had been put to him in connection with the Finnish question.[80] The Japanese Ambassador in London, Shigemitsu, reported on 30 June that it seemed that despite all the concessions made by the British the Anglo-Soviet talks would not reach any conclusion.[81] Rüstü Aras, the Turkish Ambassador in London, said on 8 August 1939 that the calibre of the officials comprising the British military mission had displeased Moscow; while the talks were still carrying on, he said that there was still no end in sight.[82]

The Attitude to the Talks in Moscow of those States not Immediately Involved

As was to be expected, Britain enjoyed the support of France in her negotiations with the Soviet Union.[83]

Turkey devoted particular effort to bringing about an Anglo-Soviet Pact. (The Turkish interest in the Anglo-Soviet negotiations has already been referred to on page 61 above). With the object of securing agreement between Britain and Russia without further delay, on 15 May the Turkish Ambassador in Moscow transmitted to his Foreign Ministry on his own initiative the suggestion that the following Declaration be proposed to the negotiating parties to aid them in reaching their decision: 'The Governments of Turkey, the Soviet Union, Britain and France will form a united front—if necessary repeatedly—against all attacks'.[84] As the Turkish Foreign Minister Saracoglu informed his Ambassador in London, Rüstü Aras on 17 May, he had brought Apaydin's suggestion to the attention of the British Ambassador in Ankara without telling either his own Prime Minister or the President.[85] At the same time, Saracoglu instructed Rüstü Aras to make representations in the Foreign Office in favour of an Anglo-Soviet *rapprochement*. In accordance with these instructions, Rüstü Aras thereupon declared in an interview with Sir Alexander Cadogan, the Permanent Under-Secretary of State at the Foreign Office, that Turkey would be content to see an agreement reached on the basis of the Soviet proposals. Should there be any kind of doubts as to the feasibility of a multilateral guarantee, however, Rüstü Aras once again drew attention to Apaydin's idea and suggested that they could agree to a Four-Power —or possibly even a Five-Power*—Declaration; or at least initially a Four-Power Declaration with which Poland would be free to associate herself.[86] Then again, the Turkish Ambassador in Moscow, Apaydin,

* *Forschungsamt:* 'Britain, France, Russia, Turkey, Poland'.

subsequently reassured Molotov that Turkey had gone to some trouble (*Forschungsamt*: 'i.e. to persuade the British') along these lines, not only in Ankara and London but also in Moscow.[87]

The attitude of every other country concerned did anything but ease the path of the Anglo-Soviet talks. As the Japanese Minister in Spain, Yano, reported on 31 May, the Polish Minister there, M. Szumlakowski, had stated that it was most reprehensible that Britain was planning to conclude an alliance with the Soviet Union against Poland's wishes; and that even if they were to succeed, Poland had no intention of allying herself with the Soviet Union, and would in no circumstances tolerate the entry of Soviet troops.[88] According to a report from Counsellor Adamovic of the Yugoslav Legation in Warsaw on 13 August, Poland expected from the Moscow talks that Russia guarantee the inviolability and security of Poland's eastern frontier; that being so, Poland would permit the Soviet army to concentrate forces on its western frontiers.[89] The assimilation of the Polish view was said to have been the main topic of the discussions held by the British military delegation in Moscow.

According to the report from the Japanese Minister in Spain, Yano, on 31 May, Rumania equally had no desire to enter into any kind of alliance with the Soviet Union or to allow any foreign military power to invade its territory.[90]

As far as the three Baltic states were concerned, Shigemitsu, the Japanese Ambassador in London, reported on 10 June that their attitude to the Russian demand for a guarantee to these countries had proven most inflexible.[91] In a subsequent despatch of 1 July, Shigemitsu stated that the attitude of these various Baltic states and in particular of Finland was diametrically opposed to Soviet guarantees and that therefore Britain could not just ignore these countries' views completely.[92]

The Latvian Foreign Minister Munters informed the Japanese Ambassador in Riga, Otaka, on 10 July, that Latvia had made a *démarche* to Britain that the British Government must respect the principle of Latvia's neutrality, to which the British had replied that this principle would always be observed.[93] But, as Munters had added, it was difficult to rely on this promise for in the very making of her proposal Britain had already injured the neutrality of the Baltic States. He added that in consequence of her proposal, which had amounted to a declaration that any country bordering on Britain, France or the Soviet Union would receive Soviet aid in the event of an attack on her, Britain had already received protests from Belgium, Holland and Switzerland.

As far as Italy was concerned, the Japanese Ambassador in Ankara, Taketomi, had deduced that the construction of ships in Italian shipyards for the Soviet Union was an indication that Mussolini was at pains to prevent the Soviet Union from joining the British and French cause.[94]

On Germany's attitude, the Japanese ambassador in London, Shigemitsu, expressed the view that the Reich would spare no effort to disrupt the Anglo-Soviet negotiations and to purchase the Soviet Union's neutrality by trade negotiations and by granting loans to her.[95]

The Background to the Difficulties in the Moscow Talks

A primary obstacle to the successful conclusion of the Anglo-Soviet negotiations seems to have been the suspicion with which the Soviet Government viewed the British proposals. Very early on in the talks the Soviet chargé d'affaires in London emphasized that Russia attached importance to concluding an honest alliance which would define both what was meant by 'aggression' and the extent of the military collaboration foreseen, to avoid in this way what Britain was aiming at—namely getting Russia embroiled with Germany in a war in which Britain would reduce her participation to a minimum or even reserve the freedom to decide what to concede and what not.[96] The Turkish Foreign Minister Saracoglu also voiced a conviction that the Russians suspected that the Western Powers planned to divert Germany's attention to the Soviet Union.[97] Against this can be set the verdict of the Japanese Ambassador in Ankara, Taketomi, on Russia's attitude in the Anglo-Soviet talks, that Russia had initially resolved to join the British camp with the honest intention of inciting the Western Powers on one side and Germany on the other to set about each other.

In pursuit of this same objective, Russia had also decided on arms purchases from the Skoda Works and an economic agreement with Germany. At that time (30 June 1939) Taketomi considered that in order to hasten the outbreak of war between the two camps, Soviet Russia would later change her attitude.[98] On the other hand, the Japanese Ambassador in London, Shigemitsu, on the same day expressed the view that the Soviet Union was vacillating between the choice of the alliance suggested by Britain and a German proposal which went beyond a trade agreement, and provided for the neutrality and inviolability of the Soviet Union, particularly as the latter would obviously far prefer not to get involved if there was to be a clash soon between

Britain and Germany.[99] A different interpretation was given by the Japanese Minister in Stockholm, Kuriyama, according to which it was primarily from considerations of internal politics that the Soviet Union had had doubts about concluding the alliance, since the Russians apprehended that one consequence would be a more lively flow of delegations to Russia after the conclusion of the pact, which would in turn increase the influence of the Western European element in Russia's internal politics and augment the anti-Stalin tendencies there.[100]

Statements by several diplomats concerned with the analysis of British foreign policy support the conclusion that the Soviet suspicion of British motives was not unfounded. The Yugoslav chargé d'affaires in London, Milanovic, stated that one reason why Britain was rejecting closer ties with Russia was so as to be able to get rid of her if the need should arise, and to preserve the possibility of a *rapprochement* with Germany.[101] In this despatch, Milanovic went on to comment that the Foreign Office was hoping to perceive from the awaited Russian reply whether the dismissal of the Soviet Foreign Minister Litvinov (*Forschungsamt*: 'on 3 May 1939') would augur any significant change in the Russian Government's attitude. The Japanese Ambassador in London, Shigemitsu, gave his impression as being that Britain was trying to play a double game—using her Soviet treaty negotiations as a weapon against the Germans, while on the other hand using a Germany-orientated peace plan as a lever on the Soviet Union.[102]

There are equally various pointers which indicate that Britain's attitude was governed by internal political difficulties. Thus Sir Alexander Cadogan, the Permanent Under-Secretary of State at the Foreign Office, declared that Britain's internal and external political difficulties militated against the Soviet proposal of a Three-Power Agreement, and that the sanction for such a proposal did not therefore lie in the hands of the Foreign Office alone.[103]

While the Opposition was exerting strong pressure on the Government to conclude an Alliance with Russia[104] and was even insisting that the Under-Secretary of State, Mr Butler, be sent as representative to Moscow, on the other hand the opinion of the writers inside Britain who had always been against such an alliance was—according to a report by the Japanese Ambassador in London—causing a reaction in Britain, to which must be added the fact that doubts were beginning to arise in Britain as to whether enough was known about the Soviet Union's true intentions.[105] Confronted with these internal difficulties, according to a

subsequent report by Shigemitsu, Mr Chamberlain had resolved to drag
the talks on until the last minute, and then concede completely to the
Soviet demands only when war in Europe was imminent. (Shigemitsu
added that he considered it highly debatable whether the Soviet Union
would really move to the British side at the last moment.)[106] This was
similar to what Rüstü Aras, the Turkish Ambassador in London, reported: the British believed that as soon as the Russian proposal relating
to an 'indirect' aggression was accepted the Moscow talks would immediately come to a successful conclusion; but that if necessary attempts
could still be made to work reservations into the Anglo-Soviet Treaty.[107]

The Development of Britain's Relations with Poland

First British Attempts at Rapprochement after the Occupation of Bohemia and Moravia; the British Guarantee to Poland; Colonel Beck's Visit to London; after the Ending of the German-Polish Non-Aggression Treaty; Conclusion of the Anglo-Polish Treaty.

After the occupation of Bohemia and Moravia, British diplomacy
concentrated on strengthening Britain's relations with Poland and, in
line with Britain's post-Munich foreign policy, on drawing her into the
system of encirclement. According to a report from the *Prager Tagblatt's*
London correspondent, Eisner, on 24 November 1938, the *Evening
Standard* reported that in face of a threatened Polish invasion of the
Carpatho-Ukraine the British Government had advised Paris to undertake no steps at present as it was inadvisable to worsen Franco-Polish
relations any further.[108] Apparently Anglo-Polish relations had been
comparatively superficial before the Munich conference in view of the
close links between Poland and Germany, and of Poland's intention of
walking out of the League of Nations. What little contact there had been
between the Polish Foreign Minister Beck and the former British Foreign Secretary Eden had apparently been solely concerned with a
British examination of Poland's attitude on some issues, without any
immediate bearing on Anglo-Polish relations as such—like Poland's
attitude to the Abysinnian war and the possibility of Polish mediation
between the Reich and France. The rumour that arose in September
1938 that Britain was planning more intimate relations with Poland was
only a rumour.[109] It was not until the British developed plans to take the

initiative, in face of the dissolution of Czecho-Slovakia, in announcing a so-called 'Collective Guarantee' whereby in addition to Britain initially France and the Soviet Union, and subsequently Poland and the South-Eastern states, should issue a Declaration, that new and more concrete objectives were laid down for British diplomacy to aim at in Warsaw.[110] The task in Poland was not however an easy one, as on the one hand Polish-German relations did not at first permit Poland to express a clear opinion, and then again Poland's attitude to the Soviet Union would have had to be put on an entirely new footing. The journey by the Parliamentary Secretary for overseas Trade, Mr Hudson, which was seen in the Polish capital as not only a trade but a political mission, as the Yugoslav Minister in Warsaw, Vukcevic, reported on 20 March, can perhaps be stated to have been the first diplomatic sortie by the British in Warsaw.[111] But, as Vukcevic went on to report, the Polish Foreign Minister appeared to want to play down the significance of the visit on account of the international situation, by ascribing to it a semi-official and purely commercial character. Even so, from Colonel Beck's acceptance of the invitation to visit London it could be assumed that Britain's endeavours had not gone entirely unrewarded.[112] That Britain shrank from no means of influencing Poland emerges from a cable from the Yugoslav Foreign Minister Cincar-Marcovic to the Yugoslav Legation in Berlin on 30 March 1939, which stated that Britain had even declared herself ready to sacrifice Danzig—i.e. to relinquish the League of Nations supervision there and give the Reich a free hand—in order to force Poland to side with the Western Powers.[113] Against which, the Japanese Ambassador in London, Shigemitsu, reported on 31 March that London and Paris were persisting in encouraging Poland's obstinate line over the Danzig issue.[114]

On 31 March—even before the Polish Foreign Minister arrived in London—the British Prime Minister announced his guarantee to Poland in the House of Commons.* The declaration read: 'As the House is aware, certain consultations are now proceeding with other governments. In order to make perfectly clear the position of H.M. Government in the meantime before these consultations are concluded, I now have to inform the House that during that period, in the event of any action which clearly threatened Poland's independence and which the Polish Government accordingly considered it vital to resist with their

* On 26 March, Poland had rejected the German proposals for settling the Danzig and Corridor problems.

national forces, H.M. Government would feel themselves bound at once to lend the Polish Government all support in their power.'[115]

The immediate cause of this, according to a report from the Bulgarian Minister in London on 31 March, was a report of imminent German action against Poland.[116] According to another London source, a rumour of a German ultimatum to Poland had been put about by the Rumanian Legation with the assistance of the British, and this had paved the way psychologically for the declaration and silenced those voices against it in the Cabinet.[117] Even as the announcement was being made, the British indicated that Chamberlain's declaration was only a beginning, and that Beck's visit would provide an opportunity of discussing whether to enlarge the unilateral British guarantee to a full-scale pact.

Thus the Polish Minister in Budapest, Orlowski, said to the Italian Minister Vinci-Gigliucci there, after Chamberlain's declaration, that London had intended from the very outset to get an agreement with Poland on the Geneva model, constructed in the spirit of collective security. While Poland was ready for this, she could not allow her position with respect to Germany to be compromised thereby. The possibility of including the South-Eastern countries was also to be discussed during Beck's visit.[118]

The granting of the guarantee [to Poland] was not welcomed at all uncritically everywhere. As Count Toggenburg reported on 31 March from London, a member of the Polish Embassy in London had told him that Poland would never have accepted the risk inherent in allying herself with Britain, had she not had to reckon with the possibility of war since 30 March.[119] In this context, a 3 April report from the Italian Ambassador in Warsaw, Arone, is also of interest: in it, he states that after some days of general satisfaction at Chamberlain's declaration, official opinion [in Warsaw] now showed signs of endeavouring to see in the declaration something less than an unqualified and absolute advantage to Poland's political interests; once again there were growing signs of Poland's innate dislike of any kind of bloc building.[120] The P.A.T. [Polish Telegraph Agency] published a statement after the declaration to the effect that Poland had no cause to give up her independent foreign policies now,[121] and Warsaw radio broadcast a similar statement on 1 and 2 April.

[On the telephone] to Ward Price, the British Counsellor of Embassy Ogilvie-Forbes [in Berlin] stated that while the guarantee was all very nice, it was a matter for some doubt as to whether Britain could ever put back into good order everything she had thrown into disorder.[122] The British provocation would call down thunder and lighting on Britain's head, and the question was whether Britain could in fact do anything at all to help the Poles. In his opinion there was a belief in Britain that when it came to the brink, Germany would give way.[123] That would not however be the case, and he had always tried to make it quite plain in London that Germany was not bluffing. The British Ambassador in Rome, Lord Perth, expressed a fear according to a despatch from the Turkish Ambassador in Rome on 20 April that the ill-treatment of the German minorities in Poland following on the announcement of the guarantee would force the Führer to take sudden action which in turn would spark off a full-scale war.

The guarantee was fortified, apparently after what were initially most complex manoeuvres, by Beck's visit to London from 3 to 7 April; this was the subject of the most diverse speculation in British and Polish newspapers.[124] To all appearances, Beck came to London, resolved, in the opinion of the Italian Minister in Budapest, Vinci-Gigliucci,[125] not to place too heavy a burden on Polish-German relations by his agreements reached with the British Government, and the Bulgarian Minister in Paris, Balabanoff, thought it safe to report on 6 April that the Polish Foreign Minister had undertaken no concrete obligations.[126] The Japanese Ambassador in London, Shigemitsu, also represented the view that there would be no development of British military support for Poland.[127] After the conclusion of the talks, the Yugoslav Foreign Minister Cincar-Markovic learned from London on 8 April that towards their end—according to information confidentially made available by the Foreign Office—the Anglo-Polish negotiations had finally inclined towards the conclusion of a pact of mutual alliance.[128] But in connection with the practical operation of such a mutual aid pact, differences of opinion had emerged, as the Italian Ambassador Grandi reported on 17 April.[129] Evidently the Polish attitude, as outlined in the commentary of the Yugoslav Minister in Warsaw, which is outlined below, had not proven entirely satisfactory to London. Vukcevic, for example, reported on 24 April that Poland did not wish to deviate from her carefully balanced line, and it was only because of the current situation, for which Germany must bear the blame, that she had accepted the security offered her by Britain. As long as there was peace, Poland would not change her policies towards any other country.

If war broke out, however, Poland would review her position to suit her own needs.

This attitude was changed only after Germany announced the annulment of the Polish-German non-aggression pact on 28 April 1939. In face of this, Warsaw now began to exert pressure on London to hasten the conclusion of the Anglo-Polish Treaty, although without at the same time displaying much enthusiasm for it.[130] The deterioration of Polish-German relations however caused the British Government, *via* the British Embassy in Berlin, to announce to the Reich Government on 11 May that in the event of a German aggression against Poland and the outbreak of hostilities between Poland and the Reich, Britain and France would intervene and Danzig would then also come under the British guarantee.[131] In Warsaw itself the seriousness of Britain's intentions was documented by the British military mission's talks with the Polish General Staff which commenced on 24 May[132] and a visit by Strang, the Foreign Office's expert on Eastern European affairs, and Jebb, secretary to the Permanent Under-Secretary of State in the Foreign Office, whose stay there from 27 May to 5 June was reported to be connected with the Danzig problem, and with preparations for signing the Anglo-Polish pact.[133]

On 10 July the British Prime Minister delivered his well-known announcement on Danzig to the House of Commons. *Inter alia* Mr Chamberlain declared: 'Recent occurrences in Danzig have [inevitably] given rise to fears that it is intended to settle her future status by unilateral action, organised by surreptitious methods, thus presenting Poland and other Powers with a *fait accompli*. In such circumstances any action taken by Poland to restore the situation would [it is suggested] be represented as an act of aggression on her part and if her action were supported by other Powers they would be accused of aiding and abetting her in the use of force. If the sequence of events should, in fact, be such as is contemplated in this hypothesis, Hon. Members will realise from what I have said earlier that the issue could not be considered as a purely local matter.'[134] This announcement should apparently have been made some days before, but had been postponed at the Polish Government's request, according to a report from the journalist Eisinger in London, until the Polish Ambassador Raczynski had returned to London from his brief visit to Warsaw.[135]

With regard to the Danzig issue, a comment by the Berlin representative of Belgrade's *Politika* on 2 July is significant: he stated that the

Berlin Poles (*Forschungsamt*: 'presumably meaning the members of the Polish Embassy in Berlin') had complained to 'the Yugoslavs' that Britain was applying enormous pressure on Poland to stir up war with the Reich over Danzig, as Britain was resolved to hazard a war as soon as possible.[136] In this context, a conversation between the American Ambassador in Warsaw, Drexel Biddle, and the Hearst representative in London on 2 August 1939 is of interest: both commented on the complete lack of responsibility in Reuter's reporting of the Danzig issue. Drexel Biddle said that the Reuter reports from Danzig were unprincipled anti-German sensationalism.[137] Eisinger suspected that the Polish request for a postponement of Chamberlain's announcement [in the House of Commons] was connected with their belief that Germany was prepared to negotiate with them.[138] There is no information available as to the real object of Raczynski's trip to Warsaw. The British press tried to account for it by publishing that the Anglo-Polish Treaty was finally to be signed immediately upon the Ambassador's return. The Treaty was finally signed in London on 25 August, after the Permanent Under-Secretary of State at the Foreign Office, Cadogan, confronted with the Non-Aggression Pact signed meanwhile by Germany and the Soviet Union, had stated, as the Yugoslav Foreign Minister Cincar-Markovic learned from London on 22 August, that the German-Soviet Pact did nothing to change Britain's attitude towards Poland: Britain would abide by her guarantee.[139]*

* On 23 August, the Yugoslav Minister in Warsaw, Adamovic, informed his Foreign Minister in Belgrade that the Polish Foreign Minister had received from the British Foreign Secretary a letter of the same content.[140]

Part III

Part III

REPERCUSSIONS OF THE POLICY OF
ENCIRCLEMENT ON THE DEVELOPMENT OF
ANGLO-GERMAN RELATIONS AFTER THE
OCCUPATION OF BOHEMIA AND MORAVIA

[*While in public the British Prime Minister appeared by his actions and his policies to have acknowledged the failure of appeasement, the private exchanges between London and Berlin showed that it was a policy in which he apparently still believed—a policy which only convinced Hitler that the deterrent element in British policy was purely a bluff. To assuage his opponents and to encourage the French, Mr Chamberlain authorised the introduction of conscription, but these and other measures were more half-hearted than stern, and seemed to Hitler to be designed to leave the door open for subsequent British withdrawal.*

The British attempts during the spring and early summer of 1939 to establish a barrier of guarantees against further Axis expansion among the small states bordering on Greater Germany and Italy, already described in Part II, merely incensed Hitler as further evidence of British meddling in the areas he regarded as a purely German sphere of interest. Apprised (and sometimes misapprised) of all these moves, Hitler concluded that it was time to put pressure on Britain by openly denouncing his much advertised policy of rapprochement with Britain.

On 28 April 1939 Hitler announced that he was repudiating both the Non-Aggression Pact he had signed with Poland in 1934, and the Anglo-German Naval Agreement of 1935, to which Chamberlain had made such fervent reference at Munich, and which Hitler's naval authorities regarded as a barrier to further rearmament. In the same Reichstag speech, Hitler still professed his continuing admiration for the British Empire, and looked forward to a renewal of the Anglo-German concord when Britain had pulled herself together and abandoned her hostile policies towards Germany. As with Czechoslovakia, Hitler intended to divide his potential opponents, and then let them fall apart without further intervention. In the event there were to be no further communications between Germany and Poland before war broke out; direct German contact with the British Government in London was not re-established until mid-August though there were important clandestine negotiations between Reichsmarschall Göring's representative and Sir Horace Wilson and Mr Oliver Stanley in July.]

The Growing Anti-German Mood in Britain

Meanwhile, Anglo-German relations had gone from bad to worse. In the House of Commons, Mr Duff Cooper made his insulting speech about the Führer on 16 March 1939.[1] In a speech on board the aircraft-carrier *Ark Royal* on 4 April, the then First Lord of the Admiralty, Stanhope, publicly announced that the British Navy was making ready and was prepared for anything.[2]

The British Ambassador's return to Berlin on 23 April, and his vain attempt[3] to secure an immediate interview with the Reich Foreign Minister [von Ribbentrop] gave British public opinion and the Opposition cause to make the most pungent attacks on Germany. People suspected that Henderson's return must be linked with the Führer's Reichstag speech due to be held on 28 April 1939, and they believed Henderson must have been entrusted by his Government with a special mission with the object of influencing the Führer's reply to Roosevelt.[4] But Chamberlain announced to the House of Commons on 24 April that no special significance should be attached to Henderson's return to Berlin.[5]

Henderson's Return to Berlin and the Introduction of National Service in Britain

As emerges from a despatch by the French Ambassador [in Berlin], Coulondre, on 26 April, however, Henderson did, in fact, have an instruction to give the Reich Government advance warning of the introduction of National Service to be announced by Mr Chamberlain in the House of Commons on 26 April, since the British Government thought it important that the Reich Government learn of the implementation of limited National Service before the Führer's Reichstag speech, and directly from official sources—not indirectly from the Press. They were also to be assured that this British step was not to be construed as directed against Germany.[6]

The British Embassy [in Berlin] was very concerned lest this intention be frustrated by some newspaper indiscretion, and accordingly made

an effort to receive the necessary instruction from the Foreign Office
with utmost despatch.[7] After British public opinion had turned to the
question of Henderson's return and the question of why he had not
been received immediately by the Reich Foreign Minister upon his
return, the British Government anticipated that it would be asked—in
the House of Commons business on 26 April—whether Sir Nevile
Henderson would have the opportunity of seeing the Reich Foreign
Minister before the Reichstag session due to take place on 28 April.
In several conversations between the British Embassy and the Foreign
Office, an attempt was made to formulate some satisfactory reply to
this Question, to satisfy British public opinion and at the same time
avoid creating further difficulties for the British Ambassador in his
endeavours in Berlin.[8]

In well-informed circles, however, as the Yugoslav chargé d'affaires
Milanovic reported on 26 April, people in London believed that the
decision to send Henderson to Berlin had been a purely tactical measure,
designed by the British Government to win as much time as possible.[9]

The Devastating Effect of the British Guarantee to Poland on the Anglo-German Naval Agreement

The Anglo-Polish guarantee agreements gave the Reich cause to inform
the British Government, in a Memorandum of 28 April, that through
its policy of encirclement the British Government had deprived the
Naval Agreement of 18 June 1935 of its basic foundation, and that it had
thereby unilaterally repudiated both this Agreement and the agreed
'Declaration' of 17 July 1937 which had supplemented it.[10]

From this point on Anglo-German relations were principally domi-
nated by the intensifying German-Polish dispute. The British Government left the Reich in no doubt as to its actions in any German-Polish
conflict, and on 11 May it directed its Embassy in Berlin to advise the
Reich Government that Britain and France would abide by their commitments to Poland under all circumstances.[11] The British Government
nevertheless endeavoured to reject the allegation of encircling Germany,
and in its Note of 28 June on the Anglo-German naval question[12] it
stressed that to describe British policy as 'a policy of encirclement'
lacked any justification whatsoever, and demonstrated a misconception
and misinterpretation of Britain's intentions.

Here one should recall the radio broadcast by the well-known

British historian Arnold Toynbee, Director of the Royal Institute of International Affairs and Professor of International History at Oxford University, on the subject of 'Encirclement in Theory and Practice'.[13] In this Toynbee stated apropos the British attempts to 'establish a peace front in Europe' that Britain was trying to secure joint action aimed at thwarting certain aims of Germany's foreign policy. Britain was said to be justified in linking up with other countries, as the very existence of other European countries was endangered by German policies. The word 'encirclement' as used in British diplomacy could only be applied to mean preventive measures for the purposes of defence, and it was only in this sense, with an exclusively defensive character, that the new peace front could properly be termed an 'encirclement' of Germany. Britain could always argue that she was perfectly justified in 'encircling' Germany in that sense, he said.

With an increasingly shrill Press campaign, the British Press and certain London political circles contributed to the further deterioration of Anglo-German relations, one consequence of which was that the British Ambassador in Berlin, Sir Nevile Henderson, reported to the Foreign Office on 25 April 1939[14] that his position was becoming very unpleasant: the Press* was making life very difficult for him.

On another occasion[15] he exclaimed, 'The King-Hall letters are damned awkward. It's heart-breaking—what on earth is the use of all my efforts after those!' As early as this attempts had begun to drive a wedge between the German Government and the German people. For example, the Japanese Ambassador in London, Shigemitsu, reported on [1 July] that Britain was trying as hard as ever to separate Hitler from the masses of the German people. Britain's policy was to divorce Germany from Italy, and to leave Germany in isolation.[16]

* *Forschungsamt:* 'i.e. the British Press'.

Part IV

Part IV

THE LAST TEN DAYS BEFORE THE OUTBREAK OF WAR

[*Since soon after Munich, Hitler's animosity had been particularly directed against Britain, a process which had increased with the increase in the rate of British rearmament decreed after Munich. In the last week of March however, the Polish rejection of the approaches which he had authorised in October for a settlement of the issues of Danzig and the Polish corridor, the very strong Polish reaction to the German occupation of the Memel, and the acceptance of the British guarantee had turned him very strongly against Poland. On 3 April he issued a directive for military planning against Poland 'as a precautionary measure' to be ready by 1 September; on 23 May, he held an important conference with the commanders of the three services on the same subject. From the middle of May incidents began to multiply between Danzig and Poland in accordance with German advice to the Nazi President of the Danzig Senate that Danzig should not provoke Poland but had no cause to show her a particularly accommodating attitude. On 8 August, after a hot exchange of notes between Poland and Danzig, the Gauleiter of Danzig saw Hitler at Berchtesgaden. There followed an equally bitter exchange of notes between Berlin and Warsaw in which the Poles made it clear that German intervention would be regarded as 'aggression'. In the middle of April, Russia began tentatively to reopen contacts with Germany, and to step up her demands in the negotiations with Britain and France for a collective security agreement: as the culmination of surreptitious diplomatic approaches by both sides, preparations were made in Moscow and Berlin for the signing of a German–Soviet Pact, in the face of which the Germans strongly believed that the British would abandon Poland to Germany's claims. The pact was announced late on 21 August, and Hitler awaited with keen interest the British and French reactions. As chance would have it, the British Ambassador Sir Nevile Henderson had some days before (and in ignorance of the German–Soviet Pact) concluded that there must be some immediate mediatory action if war was to be prevented over Poland, and on 18 August, he had cabled the Foreign Secretary Lord Halifax to suggest that*

Chamberlain should address a personal letter to the Führer. Two days later he repeated that he was convinced that Hitler had finally decided on military action to force the issue. The result of these approaches was that the Prime Minister did write to Hitler a letter of a somewhat firmer tone than he might otherwise have done in face of the Moscow fait accompli: he warned the Führer that no greater mistake could be made than to believe that because of the Pact 'intervention by Great Britain on behalf of Poland is no longer a contingency that need be reckoned with.' Unfortunately, Chamberlain did not have his heart in such strong language, for already he was asking the American Ambassador in London to get his government to put pressure on the Poles, since the British Government could not. Mr Chamberlain was the captive of the British guarantee to Poland; the futility of it all, as the Prime Minister said more than once at this time, was the thing he found most frightful. Similar sentiments were uttered by the staff of the British Embassy in Berlin at this time, and these evidently convinced Hitler and his Foreign Minister von Ribbentrop right up to the end that the British would desert the Poles once the real conflict began, so long as Hitler was careful to make the cause of the outbreak of the conflict seem the result of Polish intransigence.]

The British Ambassador hands Chamberlain's Letter of 22 August to the Führer*[1]

On the night of 22 August, the British Ambassador in Berlin, Sir Nevile Henderson, attempted to secure permission for an interview with the Führer, in order to hand him a letter from the Prime Minister. He said that he was not yet in possession of this letter, which was expected to arrive in Berlin early on 23 August, but he stated as to its content: 'It defines our position exactly—how we are bound by our obligation to the Poles, and how we shall have to fulfil our obligations should Poland be attacked. We should be ready to discuss all the problems—general problems—of interest to us and other countries in a calm atmosphere, and in the meantime, during this what one might call "preparatory period", something could be done to find a solution to the problem of the minorities. In other words, a kind of truce to allow the air to cool; during this we could at once attack the problem of the

* 'In what follows, the events of the last ten days before the outbreak of war are narrated in chronological order. The narrative is restricted to those secret sources available to the *Forschungsamt*, which consist primarily of the reports, instructions and movements of the British Ambassador in Berlin; these have not been supplemented by newspaper sources or by the *White* and *Blue Books* since published.'

minorities causing so much unpleasantness at the present time. That is
the general line the letter takes.' Henderson added that the British
Government had recommended Poland to seek direct consultation with
Germany, to find a solution to the whole problem—Danzig and the
others.[2]

At 1.10 a.m. on 23 August, the Embassy's First Secretary [Mr
Adrian] Holman contacted the Foreign Office [in London] and asked for
Mr William Strang or Sir Alexander Cadogan to be informed that Sir
Nevile Henderson was very anxious that nothing should appear about
the letter [from Chamberlain to Hitler] in the [British] Press. Even if
something were to be published at a later date, it should only be in
vague and general terms, and the letter itself should not be made available to the newspapers; otherwise there was some danger that the move
would look like an attempt in intimidation. The Ambassador wanted to
know the answer to this before he went to see the Führer, as his success
was partially dependent on this. While Holman agreed that it would be
difficult to meet the Ambassador's request, he stated that he believed
Strang to be the one man 'with all this at his fingertips'. Not long afterwards the Foreign Office informed the Embassy that Strang had agreed
to implement Henderson's request.[3]

Henderson travelled to Salzburg on the morning of 23 August and
was received by the Führer during the same morning;[4] subsequently he
telephoned the British Embassy in Berlin from Salzburg towards 3 p.m.
and instructed them to send the following despatch to London: 'I
(Henderson) handed over the letter at 12.15 p.m. I am now waiting for
a written reply. I hope to be back in Berlin about 8 p.m.—He [Herr
Hitler] is entirely uncompromising and unsatisfactory but I cannot say
anything further until I have received his written reply. Roughly the
points made by him were: Poland has been warned that any further action
against German nationals and any move against Danzig including economic constriction [wirtschaftliche Abschnürungsmassnahmen] will be met by
immediate German action. If Britain takes further mobilisation measures,
general mobilisation will take place in Germany. I assume that the
French Government has been similarly informed. I asked whether this was
a threat. His reply to my question was, "No, a measure of protection".'[5]

[Henderson in fact saw Hitler twice on 23 August, once to hand over
Chamberlain's letter, and once in the afternoon to receive Hitler's
reply. The German record shows that Hitler had a text of the letter

in front of him before he received the official text from Henderson; presumably he got it from the *Forschungsamt* as the text was telegraphed to Berlin from the Foreign Office in London *en clair* on the evening of 22 August. Henderson reported that Hitler was 'excitable and uncompromising', and that most of the first conversation was 'recrimination'. He expressed to the Foreign Office his hope that he had convinced Hitler of Britain's determination; but he could not encourage the wishful belief that this would give Hitler pause. His pessimism was hardly surprising; the German record of the second conversation represents him as arguing that Chamberlain's friendship for Germany and wish for peace was attested to by his refusal to have Mr Churchill in his cabinet. He is even represented as stating that it was 'the Jews and the enemies of the Nazis' who were whipping up hostility in Britain. The Führer, for his part, talked excitably about the thousands of German refugees fleeing from the Polish atrocities, and he implied that it was all Britain's fault: just as in the previous year Britain had encouraged the Czechs, now she had given a blank cheque to Poland to take what action she chose against the Germans. He no longer trusted Mr Chamberlain, he said: if war was inevitable, then he preferred it to come now, when he was fifty, to when he was fifty-five or sixty. Henderson had left the Führer's presence with the remark that his mission as Ambassador to Berlin had evidently failed. He was in fact already convinced from other sources that Germany planned to attack Poland during the night of 25-26 August as indeed she did plan. London also viewed war as inevitable: preparations for mobilisation were begun on 23 August, and on the 24th the Prime Minister restated his guarantee to Poland in a speech in the House of Commons. The result was that Hitler, who flew back to Berlin from Berchtesgaden on 23 August, was not so sure that Britain would not declare war, and he resolved to make one more effort to provide the British Government with the excuse for not supporting Poland he felt sure they were still interested in securing. In the meantime the final military orders for the attack on Poland were still withheld.]

On the afternoon of 23 August, the Belgian Ambassador [to Berlin] Davignon reported to Brussels on Henderson's mission [to Berchtesgaden]. He said that he now believed that this had been a final message, designed to convince that Britain would automatically declare war, a point on which Berlin was still sceptical.[6]

As emerges from a despatch from the Italian Ambassador Attolico, dated the evening of 24 August, Henderson had represented to him the result of his interview in Berchtesgaden as 'absolutely unfavourable', and had declared that in every way the Führer seemed absolutely set on war—even a general war.[7] As Attolico further reported, Henderson had informed the Foreign Office that he saw no other possibility than an immediate approach [by the British] to Poland to negotiate directly with Germany. He had ordered all the Embassy's papers to be transported to London, as he anticipated a German ultimatum to Poland on 25 August.

Henderson's Interview with the Führer on 25 August, Henderson's Journey to London and his Further Reception by the Führer on 28 August

[Hitler's current timetable provided for the military assault on Poland to commence early on 26 August, but now he was uncertain and he postponed the issue of the executive order to attack by one hour, to 3 p.m. on 25 August. At 1.30 p.m. that afternoon, he met Sir Nevile Henderson with von Ribbentrop, and began to put into effect his plan to isolate Poland. Hitler made the British Ambassador a promise that after the Polish problem had been settled, Germany would make Britain 'a generous and comprehensive offer' for friendship, or even an alliance. Faced with the growing inevitability of a British declaration of war when the time came, Hitler even seems to have suggested that she wage only a 'token war', which he would not consider an unfriendly action. He spoke calmly and with apparent sincerity on this occasion: his proposals were, he said, a last effort to secure good relations with Britain; he suggested that Henderson should fly to London and take them to Mr Chamberlain in person. But now it was London who was showing intransigence: news reached Hitler that the five-month old Anglo-Polish Treaty had actually been formally ratified, committing Britain seemingly irrevocably to war. This clearly destroyed for the moment any hopes he had of isolating Poland from the West. The report was over-taken by one of a still more disastrous setback for his plans. Mussolini said Italy was unable to fight on Germany's side unless she was guaranteed immediate delivery of impossibly large amounts of war and raw materials. Hitler was, in the words of an eye witness, 'considerably shaken'. He ordered the cancellation of the troop movements and the postponement of the attack for at least six days.]

On the afternoon of 25 August 1939, Sir Nevile Henderson reported to the Permanent Under-Secretary of State at the Foreign Office, Sir Alexander Cadogan, that he had had a further one-hour interview with the Führer that morning, and that he [the Führer] had made the British an offer. He (Henderson) was now comparatively clear in his own mind that the Führer was trying to drive a wedge between Britain and Poland. Henderson added that the Führer had suggested that he should fly to London to tell them of his offer; Henderson had replied that he considered this suggestion worthwhile. Cadogan also showed himself to be in agreement; he did not think anybody in London would object to the plan. Cadogan promised to advise the Secretary of State and the Prime Minister about it, and if there should prove to be any objections to Henderson's flying to London—which he however considered improbable—he would tell him so immediately.[8]

On the evening of 25 August, Henderson had a [telephone] conversation with the French Ambassador [M. Robert Coulondre] on the subject of their visits to the Führer. Henderson related how the Führer had not told him the same kind of thing as he had told him at Berchtesgaden, but had spoken this time of final attempts. Henderson added that he had just told Lipski [the Polish Ambassador] all about it, and Lipski could put Coulondre in the picture; but Coulondre, who was expecting a visit from Lipski, replied that he would like to pay a visit to Henderson first.[9]

Henderson flew from Berlin to Croydon by special plane at 8 o'clock on the morning of 26 August. His Embassy had made the necessary preparations for this flight during the evening of the 25th.[10]

[During the two days that Henderson spent in London, the British Government examined Hitler's offer from every angle, then formulated a reply which restated Britain's obligations to Poland, but advised the Germans that the Polish Government were ready to enter into negotiations with the Reich for a reasonable solution of the dispute. The British reply suggested further that direct discussions between the Polish and German Governments should begin on this basis.]

For the days during which Henderson was in London, 26 to 28 August, we have available a number of diplomatic reports from which we can deduce that in the Foreign Office the situation was in fact considered to have improved, and they even entertained the hope that Germany would modify her attitude and agree to make concessions.

Thus the Turkish chargé d'affaires in London, reporting on an interview he had had with William Strang, the Deputy Under-Secretary of State for Foreign Affairs, described how he had told him on 26 August that Hitler had wanted to get a second Munich; but confronted with the un-wavering and united front presented by France, Britain and Poland he had been ...... into a position from which he could not withdraw.[11] Hitler was a captive of the theories of .... To the Japanese Ambassa-dor Shigemitsu, Lord Halifax stated on 28 August (as is evident from a report by that Ambassador) that the prerequisite for Anglo-German accord was the reaching of a peaceful compromise (*Forschungsamt*: 'i.e. in German-Polish relations'). He hoped that Hitler's attitude in this respect would change.[12] The Parliamentary Under-Secretary at the Foreign Office, [the Rt. Hon. R.A.] Butler, also viewed the situation optimistically at that time and in an interview with the Yugoslav Minister he declared that Hitler did not want general war; equally, Hitler was convinced that Britain was not planning to bring about a war with Germany. That was why it was possible for a basis for joint dis-cussions to be found.[13]

[By this time, therefore, the position had been reached that the German claims on Danzig and the Corridor were not considered out-landish by the British, and both Germany and Britain were intent on negotiating their way out of the crisis. But each side thought that the other was weakening the more, and each thought the other side should make the first move. The Germans failed to realise that Sir Nevile Henderson's almost public comments on the telephone to his colleagues did not necessarily reflect the hardening mood of the Foreign Office, and the British Government believed that the con-ciliatory line taken by the Germans—typified by a series of visits from an unofficial emissary of Berlin, Mr Birger Dahlerus—showed that the German Government were 'wobbling', as Ivone Kirkpatrick minuted on 27 August; Kirkpatrick indeed believed that if only Britain remained firm, she held an 'unexpectedly strong hand'. In the meantime, Hitler had learned beyond doubt that Italy would not honour the Pact of Steel of 22 May. The attack on Poland, originally scheduled for the early hours of 26 August, had now been postponed to at least 31 August. The two days passed slowly: Henderson had promised before leaving Berlin that he was not going to play for time in the London talks on Hitler's offer, but from an intercepted telephone conversation between Sir George Ogilvie-Forbes, Henderson's chargé d'affaires, and the French Ambassador the Germans suspected that this was not true, as General Halder's diary shows: 'The enemy knows of the date (26 August) and its postponement. Britain and France hold view that it is not possible to give way so long as [German] troops on frontier. Henderson playing for time. Chamberlain shocked at personal vilification.' Five o'clock on the afternoon of 27 August, the time scheduled for Henderson's return, came and went and he was still in London. A new atmosphere of pessimism reigned at the German Foreign Office, and the German Army's Commander-in-Chief was instructed by Hitler on the afternoon of 28 August that the attack on Poland would probably begin on 1 September. For Hitler, only one chance of victory without war remained—the possibility of outmanoeuvering Poland diplomatically. He would table excessively modest proposals for the solution of the Corridor and Danzig problems—but framed in such a way that Poland would reject them, while Britain might accept. Henderson had by now returned belatedly to Berlin. Through a statement of the Rumanian Minister in Berlin, Hitler learned that Henderson had brought little with him and that war was inevitable unless some miracle happened. 'Rumania would remain neutral, provided Hungary did not commit some act of stupidity'. Henderson drove the four hundred yards along the blacked-out Wilhelmstrasse from the Embassy to Hitler's Reich Chancery, and passed through the guard of honour, which greeted him with a solemn roll of drums. While the reply Henderson had brought from London did indeed state firmly that the British Government would honour its obligations to Poland, there was also the gratifying suggestion that there should be direct negotiations between Germany and Poland. If these reached agreement, then 'the way would be open to the negotiation of that wider and more complete understanding between Germany and Great Britain.' During their interview, Hitler's statement to Henderson that the Danzig and Corridor problems were not of any real substance, was allowed to pass unchallenged. At last the rift between Germany's enemies was becoming apparent.]

Henderson returned from London to Berlin towards 9 p.m. on 28 August. The Foreign Office had advised the Embassy in Berlin that Henderson would be taking off from Croydon at about 5 p.m. Hender-

son's return had originally been expected on 27 August: the postponement of the return was attributed by foreign correspondents to a need
for Henderson to await the result of the Cabinet meeting taking place
on the morning of 28 August.[14]

The Führer received Henderson at 10.30 p.m. on the evening of 28
August.[15] Henderson had asked for the time of his appointment to be
postponed from ten o'clock to ten-thirty, explaining that he had only
just arrived in Berlin and was tired after his journey—besides which the
German translation of the British reply was not yet complete. But at
9.50 p.m. Henderson arranged a meeting with Coulondre before his
interview with the Führer.[16]

The British reply which he was to hand to the Führer had been
transmitted to the British Embassy by the Foreign Office shortly after
4.34 p.m., with the simultaneous instruction that a German translation
was to be prepared immediately.[17] [The Italian Ambassador] Attolico
reported that the British Note had been very friendly and convincing;
he had the impression that the situation had improved somewhat.[18]
But the Yugoslav Minister, Andric, learned from his Assistant Press
Attaché that Chamberlain's reply had turned out negative.[19]

[During Henderson's interview with the Führer, the latter was calm
but uncompromising, believing that the British did not intend to
go beyond the brink: he claimed the whole Polish Corridor, and
rectifications of the frontiers in Silesia. On the other hand, Hitler did
promise to consider the British Note very carefully, and to give
Henderson a written reply next day. Henderson advised him that the
choice lay between an understanding with England and a resort to
force against Poland; he could not have both.]

We have a despatch from Coulondre [to Paris] on the subject of
Henderson's conversation with the Führer.[20] According to this, Henderson had told him that the Führer had returned to the theme of his
claims on Poland and had announced that he was now claiming Danzig
and the whole Corridor and ......; he (Henderson) said he had refused to enter into discussion on this, and had referred to the British
condition that the Reich must ...... with Poland by means of free
negotiation ...... guarantee; he (Henderson) had added to this that
Poland was agreeable to negotiating on these ....

The Foreign Office instructed the British Embassy in Berlin to leak the fact that Henderson had visited the Führer to an American journalist, without making any further statement on this.[21]

The aircraft in which Henderson had flown from London to Berlin was sent back to London on the morning of 29 August with a King's Messenger and three passengers.[22] The Yugoslav Minister Andric displayed great relief when told that Henderson had not returned to London again himself, since he had been deeply shocked at the news of Henderson's previous return to London after his interview with the Führer [on 23 August].[23]

[From other Intelligence sources, and in particular from the German military attaché in London, Berlin had gained the clear impression that Britain's military preparations for war were even less resolute than the actions of her diplomatic representatives suggested. Hitler was convinced that any war in the West would be only a 'sham'. He again called the British Ambassador to him, late on 29 August, and in Ribbentrop's presence solemnly handed to him the written reply to Chamberlain's letter; the main point of Hitler's reply was an offer to draft proposals for negotiations with Poland. This offer was coupled with a demand: the German Government would 'count on the arrival' in Berlin of a Polish Plenipotentiary on 30 August, i.e. the following day. Henderson rightly objected that this sounded like an ultimatum, which Hitler denied. As the British Ambassador returned to his car, he passed through the anteroom, full of Hitler's most imposing military staff—he recognised von Brauchitsch and Keitel among them. Hitler was evidently trying the same theatrical methods as had proven so successful in February 1938 and March 1939. Nonetheless, the Germans could deduce from the intercepted conversations of the Ambassador that he was trying to do all he could to ensure that the German proposals were adopted by all the parties involved.]

On 29 August, Henderson received from the Führer the German reply to the British Note he had handed over on the previous day. Coulondre reported to the Quai d'Orsay on the same day on the subject of the conversation between the Führer and Sir Nevile Henderson on this occasion; presumably Henderson, who had had a meeting with Coulondre at 8.24 p.m., had given him a copy of his despatch to the Foreign Office about the interview to look at.[24] At 8.28 p.m. the British Embassy informed the Foreign Office that the German reply was now

available and was just being translated. They continued that the main
points were very briefly as follows: Germany would accept direct
negotiations; the Polish plenipotentiary should arrive in Berlin on 30
August; Germany was demanding the return of the Corridor and
Danzig, and safeguards for the Germans in Poland; Germany would
draft a plan and hand it to Britain.[25] The full text of the German Note
was then transmitted by the British Embassy to the Foreign Office [in
London] and to the [British] Ambassadors in Warsaw, Rome and Paris.[26]

[Henderson believed that Hitler's 'offer' was the sole chance of preventing war, and from this point on all his efforts centred on bringing
the Poles into official contact with the German Government; he urged
both his own and the French Government to advise the Polish
Foreign Minister to visit Berlin in person and at once. That evening,
he asked the Polish Ambassador in Berlin, Lipski, to call on him and
read out to him Hitler's reply, and the related parts of their conversation. Above all, Henderson impressed on Lipski the need for immediate action, since the Polish forces could not resist German
military power more than briefly. Henderson later wrote: 'I implored
him in Poland's own interests to urge his Government to nominate
without any delay someone to represent them in the proposed negotiations at Berlin.' If this last attempt to preserve peace failed, the
world would then clearly see that the blame for the war lay with
Germany alone. Lipski expressed no hopes at all, and in the event
Warsaw refused to comply with Hitler's demand for a plenipotentiary.
It is probable that Lipski did not even forward Hitler's demand to
Warsaw. Henderson began to realise that the last chance for peace
was slipping out of the world's grasp because of the stubbornness of
the Poles. Chamberlain felt the same: he told one Ambassador in
London, that frankly he was now more worried about 'getting the
Poles to be reasonable' than the Germans. The British Government
appreciated the urgency, but acted only slowly.]

30 August: British Efforts to extend the Deadline for
the Arrival of a Polish Plenipotentiary. The Reich Foreign
Minister's Disclosure of the Sixteen Points to Henderson.

In the early hours of 30 August, at 3.49 a.m., the Embassy's Secretary
[Mr Adrian] Holman reported that the British Embassy had received
from the Foreign Office a telegram in which it was stated that the

British Government was closely studying the German Government's reply, but that it would be very difficult to detail a Polish plenipotentiary to arrive in Berlin by the stipulated time.[27]

At 11 a.m., Henderson also remarked on the Foreign Office telegram referred to, and added that he could not see how even with the best will in the world it could be possible for the British Government to 'produce' a Polish plenipotentiary in Berlin that same day. One could not 'conjure a Polish representative from out of a hat'. He had naturally recommended that the matter be treated as one of the greatest urgency, but he had to admit that the tone of the reply which he had received on the previous day [from Hitler] was so categorical and stubborn—almost in the form of an ultimatum—that it would not be easy to talk the Poles round.[28]

[As it was, it was not surprising that the Poles would not supply a negotiator on time, for Hitler's demand for one was not forwarded officially by London to Warsaw until twenty-five minutes after midnight on 31 August, by which time the deadline had expired; Poland had until then only unofficial knowledge of the German demand. In the meantime, the British Government composed a long letter to Hitler containing its final terms; this was transmitted to Berlin during the afternoon, together with a short telegram to the effect that the long letter was not to be handed to the German Government until instructions to that effect had been received. Before receiving these telegrams, a number of significant telephone conversations with the British Embassy had been intercepted by the Germans.]

From their visits during the morning—Henderson to Attolico at 12.15 p.m., Ogilvie-Forbes to Coulondre at 11.40 a.m., Ogilvie-Forbes to Orsenigo [the Papal Nuncio] at 11.30 a.m., and [Geoffrey] Harrison to Berryer (of the Belgian Embassy) at 12.12 p.m.—it can be presumed that the British Embassy was endeavouring to brief the quarters concerned on the matter of the Polish plenipotentiary.[29]

At 5.15 that afternoon, Henderson received from the Foreign Office a remarkable message. The relative *Forschungsamt* record reads verbatim as follows:

'Henderson would now be receiving a number of telegrams, including one long one; there would also be a short one among them. They (*Forschungsamt*: "the Foreign Office") had all read the telegram "about the clamour [*Geschrei*]". Henderson should not get so worked up about it—the Prime Minister had personally looked into the matter and thought that the telegram which Henderson was now going to get would help him out. It had been designed to be of help to Henderson. Henderson should not interpret it otherwise, as telegrams were generally composed quite quickly. The Prime Minister had declared that he fully understood the situation, for he had after all been over there himself, so he fully understood. Anyway, Henderson would see what this suggestion amounted to, this suggestion which had been composed with the intention of assisting him in his conduct of this affair.[30]

'To this, Henderson replied that the impression he had gained was a good one. He could not write private letters now, he said, but his impression had been good. In London, the unidentified Foreign Office voice went on, people were quite unperturbed, as Henderson was aware. The Voice thought that they were on the right track now. They (the Germans) really could not expect to succeed again by summoning people to them, handing over documents to them and having them signed on the dotted line. All that was over now. Berlin must come to realise that just as much as London. Apart from that, London was still ready for that which Henderson had said London was prepared for. London just did not want to know about the other matters. Henderson, who agreed with this statement, replied that London should remain absolutely unflinching. He was just going to hand Chamberlain's message to Hitler.'[31]

A short time later, at 5.25 p.m. Henderson received the Polish Ambassador Lipski at the latter's request.[32] At 10.20 p.m., Lord Halifax transmitted to Henderson the instruction that he was not to 'talk' [handeln] until he had received a telegram that was just being composed. It would be some time before the telegram could be despatched.[33]

[Hitler's clumsy attempt to hurry the British and Poles into the trap he was setting for them was thus snarled up in the normal delays of the Whitehall bureaucratic machine. It seems possible that he really had counted on the arrival of a Polish negotiator, like Czechoslovakia's President Hacha six months before. Realising that this was not to be, Hitler during the day ordered von Ribbentrop to draft even more moderate demands on Poland—not in the belief that they would be accepted, but in order to heap greater odium on Poland when his patience was finally exhausted. In the final form they consisted of Sixteen Points, involving principally the immediate return of Danzig to the Reich and a plebiscite on the Polish Corridor—both terms long favoured by the British and French. That it was unlikely that a Polish plenipotentiary would appear before the deadline at midnight was known to Hitler from intercepted conversations (outside the scope of this *Forschungsamt* report, which solely describes Britain's policy) that the Poles were adopting deliberate delaying tactics [*verschleppen*]. While Hitler had not originally issued an ultimatum to the Poles, there was thus no profit from extending the deadline he had set. By their obstinacy, the Poles had thus rendered nugatory Hitler's attempt to separate them from their Allies. A few hours later, Hitler issued the executive order for the attack on Poland early next morning, 1 September. Henderson had arranged to see von Ribbentrop at 11.30 p.m., but he was delayed at the last moment, as he wrote in '*Failure of a Mission*' by the necessity to decode the considered British reply which had just arrived, to Hitler's offer. When he called on von Ribbentrop at midnight, the German Foreign Minister was in an unattractive mood, as he suspected that Henderson had purposely postponed his visit until midnight, knowing that the deadline for the arrival of a Polish negotiator would then expire. He read through the Sixteen Point proposals to Henderson in German— there was no point in passing the draft to the Ambassador as it had been corrected in Hitler's spidery handwriting, and, as he said, the proposals were out of date in any case as the Poles had not sent a negotiator.]

Henderson called on Reich Foreign Minister Ribbentrop at 10.30 p.m. [sic: an obvious error for 'midnight']. Counsellor of Embassy Ogilvie-Forbes told the Italian Ambassador Attolico at 10.30 p.m. that they were all sitting there twiddling their thumbs, awaiting the reply from London. The longer it lasted, the better, as they would win time like that. Henderson's visit to the Reich Foreign Minister was not a part of that.[34] We have the following report by Henderson to Lord Halifax on the subject of this interview, dated 2 September: 'In denying the B.B.C's broadcast to the effect that the German mediation proposals (*Forschungsamt*: "i.e. the Sixteen Point proposals") which were published on Thursday August 31 were not previously communicated to the British Government, the German press states that on the contrary they were brought to my knowledge verbally on the Wednesday night, 30 August, and that further they were discussed with me in detail by Herr

Sir Nevile Henderson, British Ambassador to Berlin: The Germans only
had to lure him to the telephone.

Viscount Halifax, British Foreign Secretary, with Sir Alexander Cadogan.

Hitler with the Italian Ambassador, Attolico, in Berlin.

Hitler greeting Neville Chamberlain at Munich in 1938.

If a General Election had followed Chamberlain's return from Munich (*above*) he would have swept the country. *Below:* enthusiastic crowds welcomed Mrs Chamberlain at Downing Street.

Rt. Hon. Alfred Duff Cooper: 'A frightful fellow,' said Henderson.

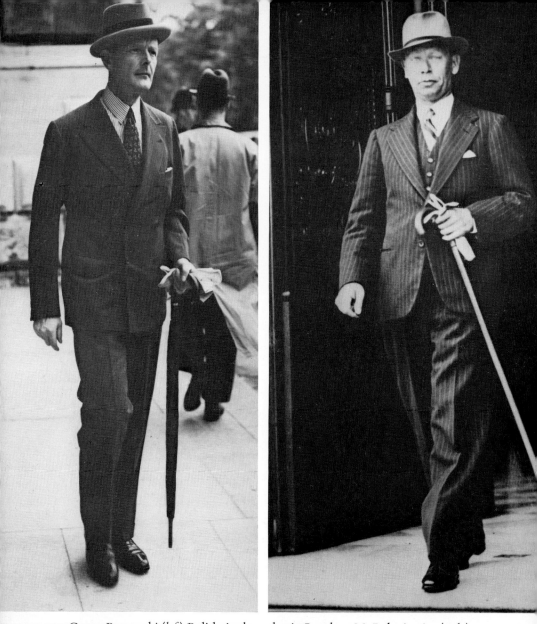

Count Raczynski (*left*) Polish Ambassador in London. M. Lukasiewicz (*right*) Polish Ambassador in Paris: Poland and Rumania were each hoping Germany would attack the other.

V. Tilea, the Rumanian Ambassador in London: an echo that started an avalanche.

sef Lipski (*at left*), Polish Ambassador Berlin: ordered by Warsaw to stall for time.

M. Robert Coulondre, the French Ambassador: left Berlin after a final row
with Henderson.

von Ribbentrop. The facts were as reported by me by telegraph after that interview. There was no discussion at all during my interview with Herr von Ribbentrop as to the details. The Minister for Foreign Affairs abruptly declined to give me the text or to discuss it on the ground that since a Polish Plenipotentiary had not arrived by midnight on August 30 (the hour at which I saw Herr von Ribbentrop) the mediation proposals had become out of date ["*überholt*"]. My answer to that was that the date mentioned in the German reply to the British Government of 29 August had in fact been equivalent to an ultimatum in spite of the Chancellor's and his own (Ribbentrop's) denials.'[35]

[After this unnerving confrontation with von Ribbentrop, the British Ambassador returned to the British Embassy. The German terms seemed to him not unreasonable, as far as he had been able to follow their content as von Ribbentrop had read them out. He summoned the Polish Ambassador Lipski, and pressed him urgently to seek an interview with the Reich Foreign Minister. Lipski ignored this request, and returned to bed. As A. J. P. Taylor presumes in *The Origins of the Second World War* (page 275), 'Every move of the last few hours had been as public as if it had been announced in the newspapers. The telephone calls between Henderson and Lipski, and between Dahlerus and Henderson, the comings and goings between the British and Polish embassies—all these were known to the Germans. They were undoubtedly known to Hitler. What conclusion could he possibly draw? Only the conclusion that he had at last succeeded in driving a wedge between Poland and her Western Allies'.]

31 August: Henderson Fears a German Attack within Two or Three Hours. He Suggests that the Poles be Advised to Suppress their Doubts on the Modus Procedendi.

Henderson tried in vain to contact the Polish Ambassador Lipski at 8.30 a.m. on the morning of 31 August, and instead informed the Polish Secretary of Embassy, Malhomme, that he knew from an unquestionably accurate source that there would be war if Poland did not undertake something within two or three hours. Would Lipski contact him as soon as possible, as there was not a moment to be lost?[36]

A quarter of an hour later, Henderson transmitted to the Foreign Office the same information for Sir Alexander Cadogan's attention, with the addition [*Zusatz*] that it might just be bluff, but that equally there was every possibility that this was no bluff.[37] He was telling this to the Foreign Office, he said, in case they should still be able to set any wheels in motion in Warsaw. The British Ambassador said that he had still not been able to reach Lipski. He (Henderson) had called on the Pole (*Forschungsamt*: 'on the previous evening') and tried to persuade him to establish contact with the Reich Foreign Minister; but as he had subsequently gone out, one did not know whether Lipski had done anything or whether he had received any instructions. He had advised Lipski to telephone Warsaw to receive instructions within the hour.[38]

At 9.05 a.m., Henderson also informed Coulondre of his fears and of the fact that he had called on Lipski at 1 a.m. during the night and urged him on his own responsibility to seek an interview, as certain proposals had been put to him (Henderson) with the remark that now that the moment had been allowed to pass, these proposals had come to nothing.[39] Coulondre took this opportunity of inquiring whether he might call round immediately on Henderson.[40]

[During the morning Field Marshal Göring ensured that Henderson was supplied unofficially with a copy of the German Sixteen Point proposals. Henderson again called Lipski, but the Polish Ambassador refused to see him; so Birger Dahlerus, who had brought the document to Henderson, and Ogilvie-Forbes went to see Lipski in person. The Polish Ambassador refused even to look at the paper: this was not the way that diplomacy was to be conducted at such a serious time as this. He was, he said, prepared to stake his reputation that the Germans' morale was weakening—Hitler's latest proposal merely bore this out. Dahlerus telephoned to London to protest to Sir Horace Wilson at the Foreign Office that it was obvious that the Poles were just obstructing the possibilities of negotiations. Wilson abruptly told the Swede that the Germans must certainly be listening in, and instructed him to put the telephone down at once.]

At 11.20 a.m. Henderson communicated the following urgent message to the Foreign Office: 'I understand that the Polish Government is raising the question of procedure before instructing [their] Ambassador to make any *démarche* here. Time is a vital point and I would suggest that on British responsibility [the Polish] Ambassador should be given instructions from [his] Government immediately to ask for an interview. The question of procedure should not be allowed to stand in the way.'[41]

[Most damning to the Polish cause was that the Germans had also intercepted the instructions passed to Lipski from Warsaw: he had been instructed 'not to enter into any concrete negotiations'. Thus when at 1 p.m. Lipski finally asked for an interview with von Ribbentrop, the Germans knew that he was only stalling for time, and at 4 p.m. that afternoon the secret executive order for the attack to begin was confirmed. When Lipski at last called on von Ribbentrop at 6.30 p.m., he merely handed the Foreign Minister a brief communication setting out that his Government were 'favourably considering' the British proposal for direct negotiations between Poland and Germany, and that a formal decision would be communicated to the German Government in the immediate future. Von Ribbentrop formally asked whether Lipski was a Plenipotentiary, and the Ambassador replied that he was not. The interview— the first between diplomatic representatives of Poland and Germany since March 1939—had lasted only minutes. Lipski had not asked to hear the German Sixteen Point proposals, and von Ribbentrop had not volunteered them to him. Not surprisingly, when the Polish Ambassador tried to telephone his superiors in Warsaw, he found that his telephone was dead. The Germans had concluded that the Polish Ambassador had wasted enough of their time.]

That evening, Henderson discussed with Coulondre a visit the Polish Ambassador had paid to Ribbentrop. Coulondre informed him that Lipski had only handed over his Government's Note; he had probably not received the German proposals. Henderson displayed great astonishment at this, and exclaimed, 'But what's the point of that? It's ludicrous, the whole thing!'[42] One and a half hours later, Henderson and Coulondre had a further [telephone] conversation, this time on the question of whether the German proposals should be accepted, if the chance was given again, or not. Coulondre formally represented the view that this would not be possible until Warsaw had official knowledge of the proposals. Henderson, on the other hand, held the view that Lipski could not even have asked for the proposals; but the announcement of the German plan had been promised to him (Henderson) as long as three days ago. How frequently he had interceded to secure just these German proposals—all he now wanted was to accept what he had been asking for all along. At this point, Coulondre and Henderson both got worked up into a very heated exchange of views, which was broken off at both ends in an exceptionally uncouth manner [*in äusserst schroffer Form*].[43]

[To a certain extent, Henderson was also helpless, as he had still not received officially the text of the German Sixteen Points, despite the German Government's promise to give him them. Only late on the evening of 31 August was he called to see von Ribbentrop's Secretary of State, von Weizsäcker, at 9.15 p.m., and at that time he was formally handed the text of the proposals. But as they had already been broadcast to the world at 9 p.m., it seemed a further insult to the British Ambassador, who now—correctly—inferred that Hitler had made his final decision.]

On the question of the disclosure of the German Sixteen Point proposals to the Poles, the British Counsellor of Embassy, Ogilvie-Forbes, informed the Papal Nuncio, Signor Orsenigo, at 10.30 p.m. that the proposals which had just been broadcast on the radio were not an Ultimatum to Poland.[44] Unfortunately, Poland only had unofficial knowledge of the German proposals, as the Polish Ambassador had not accepted the Note. Germany had now withdrawn these proposals, he said, as no Polish representative with plenipotentiary powers had put in an appearance.

[Hitler's diplomatic outflanking was succeeding, but a day too late. A dangerous rift was beginning to open between the viewpoints of Paris and London, and London and Warsaw. Late that night, the British Foreign Secretary cabled Warsaw, 'I do not see why the Polish Government should feel difficulty about authorising [the] Polish Ambassador [in Berlin] to accept a document from the German Government.' Had Hitler's Intelligence agencies secured a copy of this cable, he might have been sorely tempted to postpone the attack, for surely the British breach with Poland must now come into the open. But all was in vain, and by a matter of hours war had broken out in Europe again. At 4.45 a.m. on 1 September, German troops were to storm the Polish frontier at all points. The Germans put into effect pre-arranged plans to suggest that it was the Poles who had attacked Germany: at 6 a.m. the British Embassy was informed that the Gulf of Danzig was a prohibited area because of the possibility of military operations 'against hostile attacks by Polish naval forces or by Polish aircraft'. Göring informed Henderson that the Poles had begun the war by blowing up the vital bridge over the Vistula at Dirschau (the Germans had been unable to secure it by a special commando action themselves). At 10.30 a.m., Hitler was to tell the assembled Reichstag that he had been 'forced to take up arms in defence of the Reich.']

The Course of 1 September: Henderson believes that a Meeting between Field-Marshal Göring and Rydz-Smigly will be the only Way out. The British Government Warns that they must Abide by their Commitments to Poland.

In the early hours of 1 September, at 1.02 a.m., Embassy Secretary [Mr Adrian] Holman informed Counsellor Ogilvie-Forbes that a telegram had arrived from the Foreign Office in which, in view of the melancholy situation in Danzig, it was proposed to secure a *modus vivendi* there as already suggested, and to employ the services of the League of Nations Commissioner M. Burckhardt in the framework of these proposals.[45]

At 10.12 a.m., Henderson contacted Jebb of the Central European Department of the Foreign Office, and stated that there still existed one slender hope—it was possible that he might be summoned to the Führer's presence after the Reichstag session. Henderson reported that the Poles had blown up the Dirschau bridge. Göring had issued orders for the Polish Air Force along the frontier to be destroyed, and orders had been given for the Poles to be driven back. He (Henderson) believed that the only possible hope now lay in 'bringing the two field-marshals together'.[46] He had already cabled this suggestion to London the day before.[47] The two soldiers Rydz-Smigly and Göring must come to terms—that was the only way out.

In a [telephone] conversation with Coulondre, Henderson also mentioned his proposal that Rydz-Smigly should come to Berlin. The position was after all that Berlin was convinced that Warsaw did not want to talk, and vice versa.[48]

[Learning of the attack on Poland, Britain and France sent strong remonstrances to Germany, warning her of the consequences if Germany did not withdraw from Polish territory immediately.]

At 5.36 p.m., the British Embassy received from the Foreign Office the text of the British Note addressed to the Reich Government, informing it that Britain would not hesitate to fulfil her commitments to Poland, if the Reich Government was not prepared to give the British Government its firm assurance that it would cease all attacks on Poland and that it had made all necessary preparations to withdraw its troops from Polish territory.[49]

On the evening of 1 September, the Second Secretary of the British Embassy [Mr Geoffrey] Harrison informed Counsellor of Legation Stoker of the South African Legation that the British Note was not an Ultimatum so much as a warning.[50]

At 10.17 p.m., Henderson transmitted to the Foreign Office a report on his interview with the Reich Foreign Minister at 9.40 p.m., during the course of which he had handed over his Government's Note.[51] On this occasion, as the report was being transmitted [to London], Embassy Secretary Holman stated: 'That's how things stand at present. We may perhaps send a further telegram with a personal description by the Ambassador, from which you will be able to perceive exactly how things stand. It depends now on where Hitler is staying: he may not be in Berlin at all. I think that we shall very probably get an answer if he is in Berlin.'

[The German Government must have taken heart from its clandestine knowledge that the British Note was not an Ultimatum. When the Italian Ambassador Attolico asked Henderson whether it was an Ultimatum, or not, Henderson replied that he had been authorised to tell von Ribbentrop, had he asked, that it was only a warning. But von Ribbentrop had not asked (he already knew). The British public was not satisfied that Hitler had just been 'warned', but Chamberlain still hesitated before finally committing his country to war: the deterrent effect of the threat of war had been exhausted to no avail— what profit could now be gained by making war itself? In the House of Commons late on 2 September, the Prime Minister was still pressing for conciliation: 'If the German Government should agree to withdraw their forces then his Majesty's Government would be willing to regard the position as being the same as it was before the German forces crossed the Polish frontier. That is to say, the way would be open to discussion between the German and Polish Governments on the matters at issue. . . .' This only heightened the tumult against any policy of further conciliation. Chamberlain was warned that his Government would be defeated unless it sent a categorical Ultimatum to the Germans. In face of French opposition to this, Chamberlain finally agreed.]

The British Ultimatum is handed over

On 2 September, at 7.50 p.m., the Foreign Office transmitted to the British Embassy in Berlin the text of the statement made by the Prime Minister, Mr Chamberlain, at 7.30 p.m. in the House of Commons.[52] At the end of this they added the words, 'See my immediately following telegram.'[53]

Henderson told his French colleague Coulondre about this Foreign Office message at 8.28 p.m., and exclaimed that he did not know what it would be, but he could guess.[54]

At 12.24 a.m. on 3 September, the instruction spoken of by the Foreign Office arrived at the British Embassy: 'You should ask for an appointment with Minister for Foreign Affairs at 9 a.m. Sunday morning [tomorrow 3 September 1939]. Instructions will follow.'[55] Upon receiving this, Embassy Secretary Holman tried to contact several German offices, but without success.

At 7.43 a.m., Embassy Secretary Ogilvie-Forbes told somebody unidentified [on the telephone] that Henderson would be going over at 9 a.m., and would request a reply by 11 a.m.; if this was not forthcoming, they would ask for *laissez-passer's* and it would all be over.[56]

[When the British Embassy finally managed to inform von Ribbentrop that it had an important message to communicate to him at nine o'clock that morning, he needed little acumen to deduce precisely what was coming. He was exhausted from the strain and late hours of these last few days, and did not relish receiving a document which he knew would be disagreeable in character. He delegated the head of his personal bureau, Dr Paul Schmidt, to receive the Note. Henderson duly appeared, and transmitted the Ultimatum to Schmidt with the words, 'This is a most terrible situation, the consequences of which will be terrible. I regret it with all my heart.']

Henderson reported to the Foreign Office at 9.40 a.m. that he had carried out their instruction at 9 a.m., and had handed over the British Note to Dr Schmidt.[57]

Towards 11.20 a.m., Henderson informed Coulondre that since eleven o'clock Britain had been in a state of war; as long as the [German] troops were not withdrawn, there was nothing else she could do. He was going over one more time at 11.25 a.m. to inform the Reich Foreign Minister of this.[58]

[Henderson saw von Ribbentrop at 11.30 a.m. The Reich Foreign Minister gave him a lengthy document to read: it began with a refusal by the German people to accept anything in the nature of an Ultimatum, and added that any aggressive action by Britain would be answered in kind. The rest was propaganda. Henderson's only comment on reading this to him completely false representation of events was, 'It will be left to history to judge where the blame really lies.']

At 1 p.m., Henderson and Coulondre had a conversation about their visits to the Reich Foreign Minister. Both commented that they had taken the opportunity to 'refer to the judgment of history.'[59]

At 11.40 a.m., Embassy Secretary Holman had reported to the Foreign Office that during his last visit to the Reich Foreign Minister, Henderson had received the German reply to the British Ultimatum. The reply was eleven pages long, and its content in brief was that the German Government refused to give any assurance about the withdrawal of German troops; the whole thing, continued Holman, was propaganda designed to throw the blame on to Great Britain.[60]

Holman added that the Consulates' officers had been informed; the ciphers had been destroyed, and Ogilvie-Forbes and Harrison had gone to the Foreign Ministry to make preparations for their departure. The Germans had been very polite.

[For three more hours the telephones linking the British Embassy with the outside world continued to function, then, at four o'clock they were cut off; they had fulfilled their last function for both sides.]

Related Documents

I

INTERCEPTED FOREIGN DIPLOMATIC CABLES
SHOWN TO THE FÜHRER, 1940–1942

[Much has been written in general terms about the work of the various German decoding agencies, and their single achievements. The list which follows will put into perspective the work of two of the agencies in particular, the *Forschungsamt* (the author of the main document published in this book, *Brauner Blatt* N. 140,098) and the German Foreign Office's Deciphering Bureau (*Chiffrierstelle*).

[The German Foreign Minister's personal office, which was directed by Dr Paul Schmidt from 1939, received all the confidential reports concerning decoded cables of foreign missions in Germany and abroad, or important telephone conversations which had been overheard. The *Forschungsamt* reports received by the German Foreign Ministry were distributed to von Ribbentrop as Minister, and to the Secretary and Under-Secretary of State (von Weizsäcker and Woermann respectively at this time). Schmidt afterwards told his American interrogators, 'None of these extraordinary channels provided such a useful and regular flow of information as was supplied by the Deciphering Bureau (*Chiffrierstelle*) of the Personal and Administrative Division, from decoded telegrams and telephone conversations of non-German diplomatic personnel. The intercepted messages of the Turkish Embassy in Moscow and the American Embassy in Berne were deemed of particular value.'

[We know that Adolf Hitler had an aversion to reading the *Forschungsamt's* reports on intercepted telephone conversations: on only one occasion was he persuaded to read one, which had been specially re-typed for him on white paper so he would not know how it had been obtained (a conversation in which Pastor Niemöller had expressed himself in foul naval language about the Führer and how he intended to run rings round the Führer during a conference with him on religious affairs later that day; the report reached Hitler's hands half way through his conference with Niemöller and the other conversation-partner, after which his attitude is said to have undergone a remarkable change towards them.) However, Hitler was provided with regular series of the most important deciphered foreign cables; the reports of the German Foreign Ministry's Decoding Bureau were transmitted to him by Minister Walther Hewel, the liaison officer between von Ribbentrop and Hitler. It is thanks to Hewel's zeal as a liaison officer that we have the list that follows here, for Hewel maintained a ledger of every diplomatic document he showed to the Führer from 29 January 1940 to 16 April 1942. We have extracted for publication here only those documents obtained by interception, either by the *Forschungsamt* (the *Braune Blätter*, or *Braune Freunde*—the items with six-figure reference numbers) or by the German Foreign Ministry (the *Weisse Blätter* or *Weisse Freunde*—the items with reference numbers like T.C. 2839).

[T.C., P.C., A.C., F.C., Äg.C., Schw.C., It.C., Arg.C., Chil.C., E.C., B.C., Rum.C., Jug.C., Port.C., S.C., and Jap.C. are respectively abbreviations for Turkish, Polish, American, French, Egyptian, Swiss, Italian, Argentinian, Chilean, British, Bulgarian, Rumanian, Yugoslav, Portuguese, Spanish and Japanese coded telegrams intercepted by the German Foreign Office. The items have been rearranged according to the date on which they were shown to Hitler.]

14 February 1940
Statement by Ciano to the Belgian Ambassador in Rome (Br.Bl. No. 150,721, dated 11 February 1940).

2 March 1940
Report by Attolico [Italian Ambassador in Berlin] on his first conversations with Sumner Welles [U.S. Under-Secretary of State] in Berlin (——, g.Rs. No. 153,161, dated 2 March 1940).

4 March 1940
Remarks by Welles in a conversation with Attolico on 2 March 1940 (——, g.Rs. No. 153,282, dated 3 March 1940).

28 March 1940
Report from Belgian Ambassador [in Berlin] to [Belgian] Foreign Ministry in Brussels (Br.Bl. No. 158,437, dated 23 March 1940).

16 April 1940
Ambassador Attolico [reports] German *démenti* on movement of

troops to the Slovak frontier (Br.Bl. No. 158,437, dated 15 April 1940).
Comments of Swedish Minister in Berlin on his conversation with
Reich Foreign Minister (Br.Bl. No. 157,895, dated 11 April 1940).
'On the question of Italy's participation in the war' (Br.Bl. No. 158,399,
dated 15 April 1940).

16 April 1940
Rumours that Count Ciano is about to resign (Br.Bl. No. 158,383,
dated 14 April 1940).

18 April 1940
Italian diplomatic report on the German military operations in Norway
(Br.Bl. No. 158,833, dated 17 April 1940).

20 April 1940
Alleged imminent resignation of Ciano and entry of Italy into the war
as Ally of Germany (Br.Bl. No. 158,897, dated 18 April 1940).
Alleged report by François-Poncet on the possibility of Italian inter-
vention in the war (Br.Bl. No. 158,903, dated 18 April 1940).
[Italian Minister in] Brussels to [Italian Foreign Ministry in] Rome:
Allied plans involving Belgium. [Belgium] wants to remain neutral
(It.C. 5341, dated 15 April 1940).
[Yugoslav Minister in] Berne to [Foreign Ministry in] Belgrade: con-
centration of German troops on Dutch and Belgian borders (Jug.C.
985–87, dated 18 April 1940).

21 April 1940
The Japanese Ambassador reports on the situation in Italy (Br.Bl. No.
——, dated 19 April 1940).

23 September 1940
[Turkish Ambassador in] London to [Foreign Ministry in] Ankara:
the state of the war in the air (——, dated 16 September 1940).

19 October 1940
Alleged exasperation of General Weygand over the French Government
(Br.Bl. No. 180,361, dated 17 October 1940).
Report from Turkish Embassy in Moscow to the Foreign Ministry in
Ankara (T.C. 2220, dated 22 October 1940).

12 November 1940

'On Turkey's Position' (Braune Freunde No. 183,387, dated 11 November 1940).

[Turkish Ambassador in] Moscow to [Foreign Ministry in] Ankara: secret reports Nos. 547–558, 576 (——, dated 5 November 1940; entry endorsed 'contents extracted', i.e. for Führer).

7 December 1940

[Polish Minister in] Madrid to [Polish Foreign Ministry in] London: British treaty with Spain (P.C. 225, dated 4 December 1940).

11 December 1940

'On German-Bulgarian Relations' (F.A. No. 186834, dated 10 December 1940).

[Turkish Ambassador in] Moscow to [Foreign Ministry in] Ankara: Anglo-Spanish Treaty (T.C. 2408, dated 6 December 1940).

Draganov on interviews with leading German personalities (Braune Freunde No. 834, dated 10 November 1940).

[Italian Minister in] Tangier to [Foreign Ministry in] Rome: General Weygand's speech (It.C. 6729, dated 30 November 1940).

18 December 1940

'Spain's apparent change of alignment' (Braune Freunde No. 051, dated 12 December 1940).

20 December 1940

Despatch by U.S., chargé d'affaires on an interview with Pétain in Vichy (Braune Freunde No. 187,891, dated 19 December 1940).

1 January 1941

Magistrati [report on] Filoff's speech (Br.Bl. 467, dated 27 December 1940).

11 January 1941

Turkey on the Caspian Sea area (Br.Bl. ——011, dated 4 January 1941).

14 January 1941

Bulgarian-Turkish relations (Br.Bl.——563, dated 10 January 1941).

'Yugoslavia's relations with Bulgaria (Br.Bl.——566, dated 10 January 1941).
'Allegations about German intentions in the Balkans' (Br.Bl.——518, dated 10 January 1941).

20 January 1941
Report of Turkish Ambassador in Moscow [to Foreign Ministry in Ankara] (T.C. 2492, dated 14 January 1941).

21 January 1941
'On Turkey's Attitude' (Br.Fr. No. 190,322, dated 17 January 1941).
'On possible British reaction to the entry of German troops into Bulgaria (Br.Fr. No. 190,441, dated 20 January 1941).

26 January 1941
Bulgarian diplomatic report from London—Germany's military intentions (Br.Fr. No. 191,079, dated 24 January 1941).
Spanish general's warning to Franco about transit of German troops through Spain (Br.Fr. No. 190,955, dated 24 January 1941).

28 January 1941
'On Russia's attitude in the event of a possible German entry into Bulgaria' (Br.Fr. No. 191,217, dated 26 January 1941).
Report of the Polish 'Ambassador' in Madrid on a conversation with the French Ambassador (Br.Fr. No. 191,209, dated 25 January 1941).
[Report that] Colonel Donovan is meeting General Wavell in Athens (Br.Fr. No. 191, 242, dated 27 January 1941). [The American Colonel William J. Donovan, was on a confidential Mission in the Balkans as personal emissary of the U.S. Secretary of the Navy. See Sir Llewellyn Woodward, *British Foreign Policy in the Second World War,* p. 134, footnote 2.]
Colonel Donovan's talks in Sofia (Br.Fr. No. 191,202, dated 25 January 1941).
[Report of] Turkish Ambassador in Moscow on German-Soviet relations (Br.Fr. No. 191,046, dated 24 January 1941).

2 February 1941
Allegation that ex-King Carol is on hunger strike (Br.Bl. No.——707, dated 30 January 1941).

5 February 1941

Polish Legation in Belgrade to Polish Foreign Ministry [in London]. (P.C. 295, dated 28 January 1941).

9 February 1941

Donovan's visit to North Africa (Br.Bl. No.——480, dated 7 February 1941).

12 February 1941

Despatch of the Polish Ambassador (Br.Bl. No.——814, dated 10 February 1941).
Willkie's stay in London (Br.Bl. No.——937, dated 12 February 1941).
[Attitude of] Turkey in the event of war in the Balkans (Br.Bl. No.—— 943, dated 12 February 1941).

13 February 1941

British reactions to a German initiative in Bulgaria (Br.Bl. No.——840, dated 11 February 1941).

15 February 1941

Soviet policies in the Balkans (Br.Bl. No. ——322, dated 15 February 1941).

17 February 1941

'On alleged conditions [in] U.S.A. (Br.Bl. No. ——3132, dated 13 February 1941).

18 February 1941

Alleged understanding between Russia and Japan (Br.Fr. No. ——3400, dated 16 February 1941).

19 February 1941

The Problem of Turkey (Br.Fr. No. 193,391, dated 17 February 1941).

25 February 1941

The so-called German Army of the South-East (Br.Fr. No. 194,044, dated 22 February 1941).

26 February 1941

Balkan problems (Br.Fr. No. 194,068, dated 23 February 1941).

Balkan problems (Br.Fr. No. 194,069, dated 23 February 1941).
Balkan problems (Br.Fr. No. 194,076, dated 24 February 1941).
Balkan problems (Br.Fr. No. 194,073, dated 23 February 1941).

27 February 1941
Measures taken by Ireland against English invasion (Br.Bl. No. 194,521, dated 27 February 1941).
Alleged British counter-measures during German troop's entry into Bulgaria (Br.Fr. No. 194,464, dated 27 February 1941).
Germany's Plans to Attack Russia (Br.Fr. No. 194, 159, dated 24 February 1941).

5 March 1941
German-Russian relations (Br.Fr. No. 194,769, dated 3 March 1941).

10 March 1941
[Report] about German troop transports (Br.Fr. No. 195,416, dated 8 March 1941).

13 March 1941
Eden's visit to Athens (Br.Fr. No. 195,557, dated 10 March 1941). [Eden was twice in Athens between 22 February and 6 March. See Woodward p. 132 etseq.] Russia's reaction to Germany's invasion of Bulgaria (Br.Fr. No. 195,498, dated 10 March 1941).

14 March 1941
Landings by British troops at Fatras (Br.Fr. No. 195,923, dated 12 March 1941).

26 March 1941
Japanese-French Treaty (Br.Fr. No. 197,111, dated 24 March 1941).

4 April 1941
British propaganda against Italy (Br.Fr. No. ——382, dated 3 April 1941).

5 April 1941
Russian-Yugoslav Pact (Br.Fr. No. 198,836, dated 5 April 1941).

12 April 1941

Churchill's message to the Japanese Foreign Minister [Matsuoka] (Br.Fr. No. 199,483, dated 11 April 1941). [This message is printed by Churchill in The Second World War, vol. III, pp. 167–8; it was written on 2 April and cabled to the British Embassy in Moscow, but Matsuoka was not handed the letter until his return to Moscow from Berlin on 12 April 1941].

'On Soviet-Yugoslav relations' (Br.Fr. No. 199,458, dated 10 April 1941).

13 April 1941

Rumour of war with Russia (Br.Fr. No. 199,503, dated 12 April 1941).

17 April 1941

Britain's incitement of Moscow (Br.Bl. No. 199,753, dated 15 April 1941).

23 April 1941

Occurrences upon Matsuoka's departure from Moscow (Br.Bl. No. 199,916, dated 16 April 1941).

Conversation between Ciano and the Duce (Br.Bl. No. –31,511, dated 21 April 1941).

24 April 1941

German-Italian relations in Vienna (Br.Bl. No. 200,522, dated 22 April 1941).

27 April 1941

Anglo-Russian relations (Br.Fr. No. 200,984, dated 25 April 1941).

30 April 1941

British Intentions in Iran (Br.Fr. No. 201,231, dated 28 April 1941).

German-Russian relations (Br.Fr. No. 201,193, dated 27 April 1941).

Conversation between the Italian Queen and Prince Petrovic of Montenegro (Br.Fr. No. 201,196, dated 26 April 1941).

7 May 1941

French despatch from Washington (Br.Fr. No. ——885, dated 3 May 1941).

Exchange of information between Ciano and Alfieri (Br.Fr. No. 202,157, dated 6 May 1941).

14 May 1941
Reconstruction of Government in Moscow (Br.Fr. No. 202,516, dated 8 May 1941).
German-Russian relations (Br.Fr. No. 202,623, dated 9 May, 1941).
Spanish initiative (Vorgehen) [Turkish Ambassador in] Madrid to [Foreign Ministry in] Ankara (T.C. 2839, dated 1 May 1941).

16 May 1941
Alfieri on the Hess case (Br.Fr. No. 203,349, dated 15 May 1941).

17 May 1941
Alfieri on the Hess case (Br.Fr. No. 203,573, dated 16 May 1941).

25 May 1941
Ibn Saud claimed to support England (Br.Fr. No. 204,171, dated 21 May 1941).

26 May 1941
Japanese-USA relations (Br.Fr. No. 204,550, dated 24 May 1941).

19 June 1941
[Turkish Ambassador in London] Rüstü Aras [interview] with Butler (Br.Fr. No. 207,229, dated 17 June 1941).

2 July 1941
Both Stalin and Timoshenko stated in private interviews with foreign diplomats that the possible loss of Leningrad, Minsk, Kiev and even Moscow had been anticipated and actually assumed (—— 'Ankara T.O.', dated 2 July 1941). [Presumably intercepted material].

11 July 1941
Morale report cabled by U.S. Embassy in Moscow [to State Department Washington]: Air raid precautions, rumours about the evacuation of gold. Food supplies position (——, dated 7 July 1941).

15 July 1941

[Report] from the Turkish Ambassador in Moscow to the Foreign Ministry in Ankara (T.C. 3086, dated 9 July 1941).

16 July 1941

American Ambassador in Vichy to American Ambassador in London: Britain's armistice terms to France in Syria not acceptable (——, dated 11 July 1941).

20 July 1941

Reports of a reshuffle of the British Cabinet in near future (——, No. 211,252, dated 19 July 1941).

21 July 1941

British request to U.S.A. to watch over British interests in the Soviet Union (Br.Fr. No. 211,116, dated 19 July 1941).

24 July 1941

'On the Soviet conflict:' Japanese Government's attitude towards the [illegible] in the Far East (No. 211,294, dated ca.21 July 1941).
Panicky atmosphere in the oil region of Baku (No. 211,453, dated 22 July 1941).

26 July 1941

Attitude of Turkey in the German–Russian conflict (—— No. 211,550, dated 22 July 1941).
The situation in Moscow (—— No. 211,611, dated 23 July 1941).
Transfer of the Government to Kasan (—— No. 211,614, dated 24 July 1941).
First air attack on Moscow (—— No. 211,674, dated 24 July 1941).

27 July 1941

Report of the Turkish Ambassador in London to the Foreign Ministry [in Ankara] (T.C. 3131, dated 17 July 1941).
American Embassy in Moscow to Secretary of State Washington, signed Steinhardt (translation): Embassy in Moscow to the Secretary of State in Washington, about the first German air attack on Moscow (——, dated 22 July 1941).

4 August 1941

Turkish Embassy in London to the Foreign Ministry in Ankara: Turkish Ambassador Aras' interview with the British Foreign Secretary (——, dated 28 July 1941).

5 August 1941

[Turkish Ambassador in] Moscow (Haidar Aktai) to [Foreign Ministry in] Ankara: Turkish transports to the Caucasian frontier (——. dated 1 August 1941).

American Ambassador in Ankara to the Secretary of State, Washington (signed Mr Murray) re: pressure on Turkey (——, dated 1 August 1941).

9 August 1941

[Turkish Minister in] Teheran to [Foreign Ministry in] Ankara, signed Devez [?] Anglo-Russian pressure on Iran. British Minister's activity in Teheran. (T.C. 3174, dated 31 July 1941).

[Turkish Minister in] Teheran to [Foreign Ministry in] Ankara, signed Devez. Remarks by Prime Minister of Persia and his Foreign Minister on [Persia's] relation to Britain and Germany (T.C. 3154, dated 29 July 1941).

12 August 1941

Report from the Turkish Embassy in Moscow, signed Käzen (——, dated 7 August 1941).

[Italian Ambassador in] Ankara to [Foreign Ministry in] Rome, signed de Peppo: British pressure on Persia (It.C. 8763, dated 5 August 1941).

'On the question of British shipments in aid of the Soviet Union being passed through Persia' (——, No. 213,452, dated 8 August 1941).

17 August 1941

[French Ambassador in] Washington to [Foreign Ministry in] Vichy: translated American commentary on Marshal Pétain's speech (F.C. 17090, dated 13 August 1941).

[Turkish Ambassador in] Moscow to [Foreign Ministry in] Ankara: war situation in Russia, Japan's attitude (T.C. 3208, dated 8 August 1941.)

Turkish Ambassador in Moscow to Ankara, signed Haidar Aktai: Russian resistance and the report of American aid associated therewith (——, dated 7 August 1941).

Italian Minister in Teheran to the Foreign Ministry in Rome: Intelligence from Iraq, British troop strengths (It.C. 8720, dated 13 August 1941).

20 August 1941

British pressure on Persia (Brauner Freund No. 214,367, dated 18 August 1941).

Turkish Ambassador in London to [Foreign Ministry in] Ankara, signed Aras: meeting between Churchill and Roosevelt (Weisser Freund T.C. 3220, dated 14 August 1941). [Churchill and Roosevelt met on board an American warship in Placentia Bay, Newfoundland. Their Atlantic Charter was published on 14 August 1941].

21 August 1941

Turkish Ambassador in London, [report] signed Tewfik Rüstü Aras, 26 July 1941: Japan's attitude towards Britain, America and German-Soviet war; Indochina. (——, dated 13 August 1941. Endorsed: 'at the Führer's request shown to Field-Marshal Keitel'.)

22 August 1941

Italian Minister in Teheran to Foreign Ministry in Rome, signed Petrucci: new British move in connection with departure of Germans from Persia (It.C. 8754, dated 19 August 1941).

Turkish Ambassador in Moscow to Foreign Ministry in Ankara, signed Haidar Aktai: British intentions against Persia (T.C. 3227, dated 16 August 1941. Endorsed: 'at the Führer's request shows to Field-Marshal Keitel'.)

24 August 1941

American Ambassador in Moscow to Secretary of State, Washington, Telegram No. 1533 signed Steinhardt: Pravda article on the war effort (A.C. 8534, dated 19 August 1941).

Turkish Ambassador on Moscow to Foreign Ministry in Ankara, Signed Haidar Aktai: Anglo-Russian attempts to evict the Germans from Persia (T.C. 3243, dated 20 August 1941).

25 August 1941

Soviet offer to collaborate with Britain in military operations against Persia (Brauner Freund, g.Rs., No. 214,897, dated 23 August 1941).

28 August 1941

French Ambassador in Washington to Foreign Ministry, Vichy, signed Henry-Haye: American Journalist's despatches on morale in London (F.C. 17116, dated 20 August 1941).

[American Minister in] Algiers to State Department in Washington, signed Cole: project d'accord of 28·May considers the possibility (erwägt) of using the naval base at Bizerta, stationing German air units at Casablanca and a friendship visit by the Atlantic fleet to Casablanca (g.Rs. Algier 392, dated 10 August 1941).

To the State Department Washington, signed Cole, General Weygand on the situation in French Africa (g.Rs. Algier 398, dated 12 August 1941).

30 August 1941

Turkish Ambassador in London, signed Tewfik Rüstü Aras, 5 August 1941: report in The Times on agreement between Britain and Soviet Union on the Middle East (——, dated 20 August 1941).

Turkish Ambassador in Moscow, signed Haidar Aktai, 11 August 1941: Anglo-American aid for the Soviets (——, 20 August 1941).

31 August 1941

American Ambassador in Moscow to the Secretary of State, Washington [telegram No.?] 1570, signed Steinhardt: evacuation of all children from Moscow by 25 August 1941).

British despatch from Ankara, 28 July 1941. Alleged statement by the Chief of the Turkish General Staff, Cakmak, about the relationship between Germany and Turkey (g.Rs. No.–21519, dated 26 August 1941).

Turkish Foreign Minister Saracoglu to Turkish Embassy in London, on relations between Turkey and Persia (——, No. 215,163, dated 27 August 1941).

Eden to [British] Embassy in Washington on British aid to the Dutch Indies in the event of being attacked (——, No. 215,362, dated 28 August 1941).

Report from the British Ambassador in Ankara on Turkish reactions to the Anglo-Soviet invasion of Persia (——, No. 215,502, dated 28 August 1941).

2 September 1941

Turkish Ambassador in Moscow to the Foreign Ministry in Ankara, signed Haidar Aktai: Russian ultimatum to Persia (T.C. 3268, dated 26 August 1941).

Haidar Aktai on British intentions towards Persia (deposition of Persian ruling family) (g.Rs. ——No. 215,739, dated 31 August 1941).

Japanese Minister in Teheran on apparent difference of opinion between Soviets and Britain on armistice (——, g.Rs. No. 215,728, dated 30 August 1941).

Swiss Minister in Teheran to Foreign Ministry in Berne, signed Daeniker: situation in Persia; Russians have crossed the demarcation line. (Schw.C. 1878, dated 30 August 1941).

5 September 1941
Turkish Ambassador in Moscow to Foreign Ministry in Ankara, signed Haidar Aktai: military attache to the Smolensk front. (——, dated 25 August 1941).

13 September 1941
U.S. Ambassador in Teheran to State Department in Washington, signed Dreyfus: Shah's interview with American Ambassador; the Shah has no sympathy for the Germans (A.C. 8613, dated 7 September 1941).

16 September 1941
Turkish Ambassador in Berlin to Foreign Ministry in Ankara, signed Gerede: report from agent on German intention to attack Turkey (T.C. 3342, dated 12 September 1941).

17 September 1941
Turkish Ambassador in Moscow to Foreign Ministry in Ankara: exploitation of the newly formed Polish divisions; situation in Russia. (T.C. 3356, dated 13 September 1941).

1 September 1941
British Minister in Teheran on Russian entry into Persia (—— No. 217, 105, dated 13 September 1941).

19 September 1941
Turkish Ambassador in Moscow to Foreign Ministry in Ankara, signed Haidar Aktai: the Polish General Anders. (T.C. 3241, dated 20 August 1941).

23 September 1941
British Minister in Teheran to Foreign Office, signed Bullard: Russian and British troops in Teheran (E.C. 177, dated 16 September 1941).

25 September 1941
British propaganda guidance (——, No. 218,365, dated 23 September 1941).

26 September 1941
Turkish Minister in Madrid to Foreign Ministry in Ankara, signed Tugay: remarks of the Spanish Foreign Minister on the situation (T.C. 3389, dated 16 September 1941).

Turkish Minister in Madrid to Foreign Ministry in Ankara, signed Tugay: interview between the Turkish Minister in Madrid and the British Ambassador (T.C. 3388, dated 18 September 1941).

Turkish Ambassador in Teheran to the Foreign Ministry in Ankara, signed Üsel: behaviour of the British and Russians in Persia (T.C. 3385, dated 19 September 1941).

British preparations for construction of road from the borders of British India through Eastern Persia (——, No. 218,229, dated 23 September 1941).

3 October 1941
Turkish Ambassador in Moscow to [Foreign Ministry in] Ankara, signed Haidar Aktai: report of the Turkish Military Attache in Moscow for the Chief of the Grand General Staff (T.C. 3430, dated 24 September 1941).

Turkish Ambassador in Berlin to Ankara, signed Gerede: transportation of British war material for Syria through Turkey (T.C. 3414, dated 25 September 1941).

Situation Conference between Admiral Kelly and Turkish Deputy Chief of General Staff. Confidential communication from General Asim Gündüz about alleged German aspirations in the Caucasus (——, No. 218,637, dated 26 September 1941).

British Ambassador in Ankara, Knatchbull-Hugessen, on rumours circulating in Ankara, about British threat to send troops to the Caucasus (——, No. 218,811, dated 27 September 1941).

Turkish Ambassador in Moscow Haidar Aktai to [Foreign Ministry in]

Ankara: morale in Moscow; the Moscow Conference (T.C. 3428, dated, 27 September 1941).

Foreign Ministry in Ankara to [Turkish] Embassy Washington: American supplies to Turkey (T.C. 3421, dated 27 September 1941).

4 October 1941

American Minister in Sofia to Secretary of State, Washington (signed Earle): morale in Bulgaria (A.C. 8693, dated 24 September 1941).

[Italian Minister in] Budapest to [Foreign Ministry in] Rome (signed Talamo): Horthy's impressions of the Eastern Front (It.C. 9884, dated 23 September 1941).

Italian Minister in Lisbon (Fransoni) to Rome: British diplomat's remarks to Spanish Ambassador in Lisbon. (It.C. 9004/5, dated 27 September 1941).

French Minister in Shanghai (Margerie) to Vichy: adjustment of British policy to imminent Japanese-American Agreement. (F.C. 17280, dated 29 September 1941).

Bulgarian diplomatic despatch from Moscow on morale, military measures and the effect of the German air attacks (——, g.Rs. 219,025, dated 30 September 1941).

5 October 1941

[Admiral] Leahy to State Department, Washington, re: Marshal Pétain's reply to President Roosevelt's letter (——, g.Rs. No. 1195, undated).

Italian Ambassador in Ankara to Rome, signed de Peppo: Russian démarche in connection with the opening of the Straits for the passage of the Italian warships sold to Bulgaria (It.C. 9009, dated 27 September 1941).

Egyptian Ambassador in Teheran to Cairo, signed 'Ambassador': departure of ex-Shah and departure of French Legation from Persia (Ag.C. 15, dated 28 September 1941).

Egyptian Ambassador in Teheran to Cairo, signed: 'Ambassador': robbery of German refugees [in Persia] by the Russians (Ag.C. 16, dated 30 September 1941).

British Government's intention to send deposed Shah to Mauritius (—— No. 219,122, dated 30 September 1941).

6 October 1941

Secretary of State, Washington, to American Ambassador in Moscow, signed Hull: President Roosevelt's Note to Stalin re: aid (A.C. 8707, dated 29 September 1941).

British Ambassador in Teheran [to Foreign Office in London]: interview with Prime Minister Furuglu on the plan for an Alliance between Persia, Britain and the Soviet Union (——, g.Rs. No. 219,123, dated 1 October 1941).

'Differences between the British and the Soviets in Persia' (——, g.Rs. No. 219,534, dated 3 October 1941).

7 October 1941

'Editorial treatment of the Führer's speech by American press representatives in Berlin' (——, No. 219,601, dated 4 October 1941).

Italian Ambassador in Tokio (Indelli) to [Foreign Ministry in] Rome: dissatisfaction of Japanese public opinion over the talks with America. (It.C. 9032, dated 1 October 1941).

8 October 1941

Turkish Ambassador in London (Aras) to [Foreign Ministry in] Ankara: Turkish supplies of chrome to Germany and Britain (T.C. 3437, dated 24 September 1941).

8 October 1941

[Italian] Foreign Ministry, Rome to [Italian] Ambassador, Tokyo: North American relations with Japan (It.C. 9018, dated 28 September 1941).

Britain's plans against Afghanistan (——, g.Rs. Nr. 219,008, dated 30 September 1941).

Ditto: India considers the offensive against Afghanistan a grave error, rejects joint action with Russia (——, g.Rs. Nr. 219,117 dated 30 September 1941).

Polish Minister in Teheran to [Polish] Foreign Ministry in London (signed Karszo-Siedlewski): behaviour of Soviet troops in Iran (P.C. 620, dated 1 October 1941).

Turkish Ambassador in Moscow (Haidar Aktai) to [Foreign Ministry in] Ankara: the Moscow Conference. [A British delegation headed by Lord Beaverbrook had arrived in Moscow on 28 September, to regulate the arrangements for supplies to Russia until June, 1942. See Sir Llewellyn

Woodward, *British Foreign Policy in the Second World War*, pp. 155–160.]
(T.C. 3451, dated 2 October 1941).
Turkish Ambassador in London (Aras) to [Foreign Ministry in] Ankara:
deliveries of chrome from Turkey. (T.C. 3455, dated 2 October 1941).
Foreign Minister in Rome to the [Italian] Embassy in Washington:
Myron [C.] Taylor's special mission re: Pope. (It.C. 9037, dated 3
October 1941).

9 October 1941

Turkish Ambassador in Moscow (Haidar Aktai) to [Foreign Ministry
in] Ankara: Batum population detailed to construct air raid shelters.
Low morale of population. (T.C. 3456, dated 4 October 1941).
Turkish Ambassador in Teheran to [Foreign Ministry in] Ankara,
(signed Üsel): the situation in Persia (T.C. 3459, dated 4 October 1941).
Italian Ambassador in Ankara (de Peppo) to [Foreign Ministry in]
Rome: statements of the Turkish Consul-General at Basra (It.C. 9051,
dated 5 October 1941).

10 October 1941

Turkish Ambassador in Teheran to [Foreign Ministry in] Ankara:
troop movements in Iran (T.C. 3464, dated 1 October 1941).
[Persian] Foreign Ministry, Teheran, to Persian Ambassador in Moscow
(signed Soheily): confiscation of Persian police force's weapons by
Russians (Iran.C. 691, dated 5 October 1941).

11 October 1941

Italian Minister in Sofia to [Foreign Ministry in] Rome (signed Magistrati): escape of Grand Mufti (It.C. 9054, dated 6 October 1941.)

12 October 1941

[Persian] Foreign Ministry in Teheran to [Embassy] in Moscow,
(signed Soheily): uncertainty and unrest in Persia. Confiscation of
Persian police force's weapons by Russians (Iran.C. 693/691, dated 6
and 5 October 1941).
Situation in Persia: machinations of the Russian occupation forces;
French representation; Persian revolutionary movement (——, g.Rs.
No. 220,278, dated 10 October 1941).
[Summary report on:] Anglo-Soviet tension in Persia. Eden's conver-
sation with Maisky. (——, g.Rs. No. 220,342, dated 10 October 1941)

15 October 1941

Turkish Ambassador in Moscow (Haidar Aktai) to [Foreign Ministry] in Ankara: situation in Russia after collapse of Soviet front (T.C. 3496, dated 10 October 1941).

Italian Minister in Kabul (Anaroni) to [Foreign Ministry in] Rome: situation in India (It.C. 9074, dated 10 October 1941).

Jugoslav Minister Gavrilovic on the situation in Moscow (——, g.Rs. No. 220, 471 dated 12 October 1941).

[Telegram from] Bismarck, Rome: decoded telegram of American Embassy in Moscow to the Defence Department, Washington, 5 October 1941, re: arms deliveries to the Soviets (Rome telegram No. 2515, dated 13 October 1941).

17 October 1941

Foreign Ministry in Ankara to [Turkish] Ambassador in Moscow: Maisky's views on the war situation. (T.C. 3502, dated 13 October 1941).

20 October 1941

Turkish Ambassador in Teheran (Üsel) to [Foreign Ministry in] Ankara: situation in Persia (T.C. 3508 dated 11 October 1941).

Chilean Ambassador in Berlin (Barros) to [Foreign Ministry in] Santiago: attempt to influence Chilean Government in Germany's favour (Chil.C. 185, dated 17 October 1941).

[Turkish Embassy in] Moscow (signed Erdschin) to [Foreign Ministry in] Ankara: situation in Moscow (T.C. 3548, dated 18 October 1941).

21 October 1941

[Turkish Ambassador in] Washington to [Foreign Ministry in] Ankara: relations between America and Japan (T.C. 3550 dated 20 October 1941).

[Turkish Ambassador in] London to [Foreign Ministry in] Ankara: Churchill on the development of the war (T.C. 3555 dated 23 October 1941)

22 October 1941

Report by Japanese Ambassador on situation in Moscow (——, No. 221,278 dated 19 October 1941).

Turkish Ambassador in Tokyo to [Foreign Ministry in] Ankara: Japan's new policy. (T.C. 3523, dated 19 October 1941).

25 October 1941

Polish Minister in Teheran to [Polish Foreign Ministry in] London: British and Soviet troops in Persia (P.C. 651 dated 20 October 1941).

26 October 1941

American Ambassador in Kuibyshev* to Washington, (signed Steinhardt): present telegraphic address of American Embassy in Soviet Union. (A.C. 8799, dated 21 October 1941).

28 October 1941

Yugoslav Minister Gavrilovic on the situation in Moscow (——, No. 222,008, dated 24 October 1941).

Turkish report on Moscow, the evacuation of machinery (——, No. 222,062, dated 25 October 1941).

Italian diplomatic report from Bucharest about Soviet retreat and evacuation steps (——, No. 222,063, dated 25 October 1941).

Polish Ambassador in Kuibyshev to [Polish Foreign Ministry in] London: the situation in the Soviet Union (P.C. 660/659, dated 24 October 1941).

[Turkish Ambassador in] Kuibyshev (Haidar Aktai) to [Foreign Ministry in] Ankara: conditions at Kuibyshev (T.C. 3553, dated 24 October 1941).

[Italian Foreign Minister in] Berlin to [Foreign Ministry in] Rome, signed Ciano: Führer's conversation with Ciano [on 25 October] (It.C. 9158, dated 25 October 1941).

29 October 1941

[Turkish Ambassador in] Moscow to [Foreign Ministry in] Ankara: military situation in Russia (T.C. 3478, dated 9 October 1941).

30 October 1941

French Governor-General in Indochina to Vichy: subversive activity of Japanese secret service in Annam (F.C. 17, 424 dated 27 October 1941).

31 October 1941

Bulgarian report on the situation in Moscow (——, No. 222,398, dated 28 October 1941).

* [The Diplomatic Corps was temporarily evacuated here from Moscow.]

[American Ambassador in] Kuibyshev to [State Department] Washington: poor accommodation and provisioning of American Embassy in Kuibyshev. (A.C. 8830, dated 29 October 1941).

Japanese Minister in Helsinki to [Foreign Ministry in] Tokyo: declaration of Finnish President Ryti (J.C. 6073, dated 28 October 1941).

Bulgarian Minister in Rome to [Foreign Ministry in] Sofia: reception of Roosevelt's speech in Italy (B.C. 119, dated 29 October 1941).

French Minister in Ottawa to Vichy: Canadian journalists' report on situation in Britain (F.C. 17443, dated 30 October 1941).

2 November 1941

Turkish Minister in Stockholm to [Foreign Ministry in] Ankara: interview of Turkish Minister with Russian Counsellor of Embassy and Military Attache. (T.C. 3567, dated 30 October 1941).

[Turkish Ambassador in] Tokyo to [Foreign Ministry in] Ankara (signed Tek): Turkish Ambassador's interview with Japanese Foreign Minister (T.C. 3569, dated 31 October 1941).

5 November 1941

[Foreign office in] London to [British Embassy in] Stockholm: guidance for the press (E.C. 288, dated 31 October 1941).

[Turkish Ambassador in] Tokyo to [Foreign Ministry in] Ankara: Japanese warning to USA (T.C. 3570, dated 2 November 1941).

Despatch of a Military Mission to Irak (——, No. 223,185, dated 4 November 1941).

12 November 1941

Argentine Minister in Budapest to [Foreign Ministry in] Buenos Aires: conversation with the Hungarian Foreign Minister (Arg. C. 182, dated 6 November 1941).

Turkish Ambassador in Kuibyshev to [Foreign Ministry in] Ankara: British and American intentions in Russia and Persia (T.C. 3591/2, dated 6 November 1941).

French Ambassador in Washington (Henry-Haye) to Vichy: despatch of K——s [cruiser?] to USA, policies towards France and Indochina (F.C. 17450, dated 6 November 1941).

14 November 1941

Japanese report on military parade in Kuibyshev on 7 November (——, No. 224,120 dated 12 November 1941).

15 November 1941

[Turkish Ambassador in] Kuibyshev to [Foreign Ministry in] Ankara; Litvinov's nomination as Soviet Ambassador in Washington (T.C. 3603, dated 8 November 1941).

17 November 1941

French Foreign Ministry in Vichy to [French] Ambassador in Tokyo: instructions for an interview with Togo (F.C. 17501, dated 9 November 1941).

Turkish Ambassador in Kuibyshev to [Foreign Ministry in] Ankara: re British Ambassador [Sir Stafford] Cripps (T.C. 3608, dated 9 November 1941).

Ankara to Kuibyshev: October Festival in Moscow, and the military situation (T.C. 3612, dated 11 November 1941).

[Turkish Ambassador in] Kuibyshev to [Foreign Ministry in] Ankara: news from Batum. (T.C. 3613, dated 11 November 1941).

18 November 1941

[Turkish Embassy in Kuibyshev to Foreign Ministry in Ankara?] Parade on Revolution Anniversary: Military Attache on Russian war material (T.C. 3618, dated 10 November 1941).

19 November 1941

British Ambassador in Moscow, Cripps, on Anglo-Russian relations in Persia (——, Nr. 224,592, dated 15 November 1941).

24 November 1941

The reasons for General Weygand's recall: changes in Africa (——, 225,351 dated 22 November 1941).

Anglo-Russian preparations to bring Russian tonnage out of the Black Sea (——, 225,353, dated 22 November 1941).

Visit by Rumanian Deputy Prime Minister to Berlin (——, 225,425, dated 22 November 1941).

29 November 1941

Turkish Ambassador in Moscow to [Foreign Ministry in] Ankara: situation around Moscow (T.C. 3658, dated 25 November 1941).

Turkish Ambassador in London to [Foreign Ministry] in Ankara: Turkish Ambassador's interview with British Foreign Secretary (T.C. 3667, dated 16 November 1941).

30 November 1941

Turkish Ambassador in Kuibyshev to [Foreign Ministry in] Ankara: conversation between Stalin and Sikorski (T.C. 3653, dated 19 November 1941).

American Minister in Helsinki to [State Department] Washington: food supplies from American Red Cross to the population of Leningrad (A.C. 8950, dated 21 November 1941).

Turkish Ambassador in Kuibyshev to [Foreign Ministry in] Ankara: situation on eastern front; the Red Army; war industries (T.C. 3668, dated 22 November 1941).

[Italian] Foreign Ministry, Rome, to [Italian] Embassy, Washington: the mood in USA towards Britain (It.C. 9369, dated 24 November 1941).

Finnish Prime Minister's emphatic demand to Witting to return by 28 November (——, No. 225,780, dated 25 November 1941).

British Economic Warfare directive for event of war with Japan (——, No. 226,156, dated 28 November 1941).

2 December 1941

Turkish Ambassador in Washington to [Foreign Ministry in] Ankara: American-Japanese negotiations (T.C. 3685, dated 27 November 1941).

6 December 1941

Yugoslav Minister in Kuibyshev to Foreign Minister [of Yugoslav government in exile] in London: Russians are laying mines under all vital points in Moscow (Jug.C. 1768, dated 27 November 1941). [This was precisely the reason why Hitler had ordered *OKW* not to accept a capitulation of Moscow, if offered: see *OKW* War Diary, and signal from *OKH* to Army Group Centre, 12 October 1941].

[Turkish Ambassador in Kuibyshev to Foreign Ministry in Ankara?] Situation in and around Moscow (T.C. 3696, dated 29 November 1941).

7 December 1941

Italian Ambassador in Ankara [de Peppo] to [Foreign Ministry in] Rome: Turkish attitude towards Soviet Russia, and the New Order in Europe (It.C. 9430, dated 3 December 1941).

9 December 1941

[Turkish Ambassador in] Kuibyshev to [Foreign Ministry in] Ankara:

activation of new armies in Russia; article in 'Pravda' (T.C. 3732, dated 4 December 1941).

10 December 1941

[Turkish Ambassador in] Kuibyshev to [Foreign Ministry in] Ankara: the situation in Batum (T.C. 3740 dated 6 December 1941).

[Polish Ambassador in] Kuibyshev to [Polish Foreign Ministry in] London: conversation between Sikorski and Stalin (Poln.C. 746, dated 7 December 1941).

[Italian representative] Smyrna to [Foreign Ministry] Rome: troop concentrations in Irak and Palestine (It.C. 9454, dated 8 December 1941).

[Summary report] on the outbreak of hostilities between Japan and America (——, No. 227,291, dated 8 December 1941).

16 December 1941

[Turkish Ambassador in] Kuibyshev (Haidar Aktai) to [Foreign Ministry in] Ankara: situation on the German-Russian front (T.C. 3744, dated 8 December 1941).

[Turkish Ambassador in] Kuibyshev to [Foreign Ministry in] Ankara: Stalin pleased with situation at the front (T.C. 3749, dated 10 December 1941).

French Minister in Bangkok to Vichy: reasons for Thailand's cessation of resistance to Japan (F.C. 17672, dated 10 December 1941).

[U.S. Secretary of State in] Washington to [Foreign Ministry in] Vichy, signed [Cordell] Hull: message from Roosevelt to Pétain (A.C. 9046, dated 10 December 1941).

Swiss Minister in Lisbon to [Foreign Ministry in] Berne: situation in Portugal (Schw.C. 2111, dated 11 December 1941).

[Summary report] on the attitude of the Soviet Union in the Pacific War (——, No. 228,033, dated 13 December 1941).

Haidar Aktai on Anglo-Russian negotiations (——, No. 228,060, dated 14 December 1941).

16 December 1941

[Foreign Ministry in] Vichy to [French Minister in] Rio de Janeiro: three American Notes to the French Government. France's attitude to the new conflict [between Japan and the Allies]. French ships off the Antilles. Non-employment of French Fleet (F.C. 17673, dated 13 December 1941).

17 December 1941

Turkish Ambassador in Washington to [Foreign Ministry in] Ankara: Litvinov's formal address on handing over the accompanying document (T.C. 3771, dated 10 December 1941).

Turkish Ambassador in Kuibyshev to [Foreign Ministry in] Ankara: imminent interview of British Foreign Secretary with Stalin (T.C. 3790, dated 12 December 1941). [Mr Eden saw Stalin and Molotov on 16 December: see Woodward, *op. cit.*, pp. 190–93.]

18 December 1941

[Turkish Ambassador in] Kuibyshev to [Foreign Ministry in] Ankara, signed Haidar Aktai: British-American-Soviet cooperation (T.C. 3750, dated 10 December 1941).

Portuguese Minister in Rio de Janeiro to [Foreign Ministry in] Lisbon: Brasil, Argentina and Chile will not declare war (Port.C. 62, dated 15 December 1941).

19 December 1941

[Turkish Ambassador in] Kuibyshev to [Foreign Ministry in] Ankara: Japan's desire to stay neutral towards Russia (T.C. 3745, dated 10 December 1941).

Japanese-Soviet relations (——, No. 228,334, dated 16 December 1941). France's attitude towards Germany (——, No. 228,378, dated 16 December 1941).

20 December 1941

Swiss Minister in Madrid to [Foreign Ministry in] Berne: American interests represented in Madrid by Swiss (Schw.C. 2117, dated 16 December 1941).

Swiss Minister in London to [Foreign Minister in] Berne: Anglo-Russian Declaration. Repair depot in Italian East Africa (Schw.C. 2125). Bulgarian report on shooting of German prisoners of war (——, No. 228,464 dated 17 December 1941).

21 December 1941

Situation in North-East Asia (——, Nr. 228,494, dated 18 December 1941).

Anglo-Soviet cooperation (——, No. 228,467, dated 18 December 1941).

22 December 1941

Polish Foreign Ministry in London to [Polish] Ambassador in Kuibyshev: the purpose of Eden's visit to Moscow (P.C. 763, dated 13 December 1941).

American Ambassador in Kuibyshev to [State Department in] Washington: optimistic Russian army despatches (A.C. 9074, dated 14 December 1941).

Italian Minister in Dublin to Italian Minister in Berne: depression in London official circles after Japan's entry into war (It.C. 9543 dated 19 December 1941).

Italian Ambassador in Santiago to [Foreign Ministry in] Rome: Chile's attitude unaffected by America (It.C. 9540, dated 18 December 1941).

French Minister in Bangkok to French Ambassador in Berne: assessment of British policy in the Far East (F.C. 17707, dated 17 December 1941).

French Foreign Ministry to French Ambassador in Peping: emphatic stress on French neutrality in the Pacific towards Chungking (F.C. 17732, dated 18 December 1941).

French Foreign Ministry to French Ambassador in Rio: Petain's gratitude to U.S.A. for their intention to maintain *status quo* in the West, and for economic aid to North Africa (F.C. 17738, dated 19 December 1941).

[Turkish Foreign Ministry in] Ankara to [Turkish Ambassador in] Teheran: Kurdish uprising in Persia (T.C. 3795 dated 18 December 1941).

[Turkish Foreign Ministry in] Ankara to [Turkish Ambassador in] London: non delivery of fifty American aircraft to Turkey (T.C. 3799, dated 19 December 1941).

23 December 1941

Turkish Minister in Stockholm [to Foreign Ministry in Ankara?]: statement of Russian Minister Katz in Stockholm (T.C. 3800, dated 10 December 1941).

[Summary report on] Eden's visit to Teheran, and that of General Sikorski (——, No. 228,852, dated 20 December 1941).

[Summary report on] Soviet-Japanese relations (——, No. 228,826, dated 20 December 1941).

[Summary report on] Anglo-American War Council (——, No. 228, 894, dated 20 December 1941).

24 December 1941

Egyptian Ambassador in Teheran to Cairo: visit of Sikorski and Anders; military talks in Teheran (Äg.C. 50, dated 19 December 1941).

26 December 1941

Polish Ambassador in Kuibyshev to [Polish] Minister in Cairo: Eden's departure from Moscow (P.C. 770, dated 20 December 1941).

[Summary report on] Conference between Ciano and [Admiral] Darlan (——, No. 229,189, dated 24 December 1941).

30 December 1941

Turkish Ambassador in Berlin to [Foreign Ministry in] Ankara: change-over in German High Command. (T.C. 3837, dated 22 December 1941).

Turkish Ambassador in London to [Foreign Ministry in] Ankara: the Turkish Ambassador in London on the general situation (T.C. 3841, dated 25/26 December 1941).

Yugoslav Ambassador in Ankara to [Yugoslav] Foreign Ministry in London: von Papen's interview with Saracoglu and audience with Inönü (Jug.C. 1798, dated 27 December 1941).

Foreign Ministry in Rome to Italian Ambassador in Santiago: joint action with Vatican to ensure continued neutrality of South America (Ital.C. 9614, dated 29 December 1941).

Italian Ambassador in Santiago to [Foreign Ministry in] Rome: Chile will not sever diplomatic relations with the Axis (It.C. 9609, dated 29 December 1941).

1 January 1942

Italian Ambassador in Tokyo to [Foreign Ministry in] Rome: Japan's intentions of mediating for peaceful settlement in German-Russian conflict (It.C. 9590 dated 27 December 1941).

[French Ambassador in] Washington to [Foreign Ministry in] Vichy: first session of the Anglo-American War Council in the White House (F.C. 17769, dated 23 December 1941).

3 January 1942

[Summary report:] Britain desires a French declaration of neutrality in the Indian Ocean (——, No. 229,583, dated 2 January 1942).

6 January 1942

[Turkish Ambassador in] Moscow to [Foreign Ministry in] Ankara:

situation in and around Moscow (T.C. 3848, dated 23 December 1941). [Turkish Ambassador in] Kuibyshev to [Foreign Ministry in] Ankara: conclusions reached in the talks between Eden and Stalin (T.C. 3849, dated 1 January 1942).

[Summary report on:] Sino-Japanese conflict (——, No. 229,696, dated 3 January 1942).

8 January 1942

Turkish Ambassador in Washington to [Foreign Ministry in] Ankara: Russian demands for a Moscow conference (T.C. 3874, dated 5 January 1942).

13 January 1942

[Yugoslav Minister in] Berne to Yugoslav Foreign Ministry in London, signed Juristić: Gafencu in Berne on secret mission for Rumanian Court (——, dated 4 December, received 29 December 1941).

Turkish Consul in Moscow to Foreign Ministry in Ankara: effect of German air attacks on and around Moscow (T.C. 3852, dated 30 December 1941).

Foreign Office in London to [British Embassy in] Cairo: British news from the Dominions (E.C.5, dated 2 January 1942).

[French Ambassador in] Asunción to [Foreign Ministry in] Vichy: non belligerence of Paraguay (F.C. 17779, dated 3 January 1942).

[French Minister in] Stockholm to [Foreign Ministry in] Vichy, signed Vaux Saint Cyr: Sweden fears possible massive invasion of Norway by the British (F.C. 17798, dated 3 January 1942).

Protest of American chargé d'affaires in Kuibyshev against article in 'Pravda' (——, No. 229734, dated 5 January 1942).

[Summary report on:] Doubts in London as to Turkey's will to resist (——, No. 229,791, dated 5 January 1941).

Bulgarian report from Kuibyshev on military operations in the East and the internal political situation (——, No. 229,950 dated 7 January 1942).

[Summary report on:] Morale in the U.S.A. (——, No. 230,041, dated 5 January 1942).

14 January 1942

Turkish Ambassador in London to [Foreign Ministry in] Ankara: Churchill's talks in Washington on the apportioning of the overall command (T.C. 3872, dated 5 January 1942).

Bulgarian representative in Moscow to the Foreign Ministry in Sofia: conditions in Moscow (B.C. 215, dated 5 January 1942).

Italian Minister in Bucharest to [Foreign Ministry in] Rome: British offer to Rumania to guarantee her old Transylvanian frontiers (It.C. 9672, dated 7 January 1942).

[Turkish Ambassador in London to Foreign Ministry in Ankara?] Conversation of Turkish Ambassador Aras with [General] de Gaulle, on the situation in Russia (T.C. 3884, dated 7 January 1942).

Turkish diplomatic report on Germany's attitude towards Portugal (——, No. 230,120, dated 8 January 1942).

16 January 1942

Swiss Minister in Washington to [Foreign Ministry in] Berne: situation and morale in U.S.A. (Schw.C. 2176, dated 9 January 1942).

18 January 1942

Foreign Office in London to Consul-General, Leopoldville: guidance on the week's news. The Pacific, Russia, Libya, Eden's visit to Moscow, the war at sea (E.C. 16, dated 8 January 1942).

British corn shortage in Middle East (——, No. 230,799, dated 15 January 1942).

Conversation of [American] Ambassador [William C.] Bullitt with Turkish Ambassador Taray (——, No. 230,996, dated 17 January 1942).

19 January 1942

State Department in Washington to [American] Minister in Cairo: supply difficulties for British forces and civil population in Middle East (A.C. 9132, dated 9 January 1942).

[Turkish] Foreign Ministry in Ankara to Turkish Ambassador in Teheran: Stalin's statement on the Moscow Talks (T.C. 3895, dated 10 January 1942).

21 January 1942

Foreign Ministry in Ankara to [Turkish Ambassador in] Kuibyshev: report of Moscow Consulate on bomb damage, petrol shortage, fighting for Moskaisk, planned surprise attack on Kharkov (T.C. 3910, dated 13 January 1942). [The Soviet counter-offensive began against Kharkov on 9 May, under the command of Marshal Timoshenko].

Turkish Consul in Batum on military measures, arrest of four Russian naval officers (——, No. 231,258, dated 20 January 1942).

Turkish report from Moscow on the military situation at the end of 1941, and the plans and preparations of Russian Army Command (——, No. 231,259, dated 20 January 1942).

23 January 1942

Turkish Ambassador in Kuibyshev to Foreign Ministry in Ankara: report from Batum (T.C. 3925, dated 18 January 1942).

[Turkish Ambassador in] Kuibyshev to [Foreign Ministry in] Ankara: air raid warning in Batum, hospital transports (T.C. 3929, dated 20 January 1942).

Circular of Turkish Foreign Ministry to Ambassador in Vichy, on war situation: remarks of de Gaulle repeated (——, No. 231,444, dated 21 January 1942).

[Turkish Ambassador in] Kuibyshev to [Foreign Ministry in] Ankara: military situation in Russia; [statements of] Head of British Military Mission on the military situation (T.C. 3955, dated 23 January 1942).

24 January 1942

Bulgarian [Minister] in Moscow to [Foreign Ministry in] Sofia, signed Tileff: food situation in Russia (B.C. 228, dated 19 January 1942).

25 January 1942

Turkish Consul in Moscow to Foreign Minister in Ankara: food situation in Moscow; military situation; activation of Polish divisions (T.C. 3937, dated 18 January 1942).

[Turkish Ambassador in] London to [Foreign Ministry in] Ankara, signed Aras: British Foreign Secretary's attempt at cordiality towards Turkish Ambassador (T.C. 3934, dated 16 January 1942).

[Turkish Ambassador in] London to [Foreign Ministry in] Ankara: Eden's interview with the Turkish Ambassador, British deliveries to Turkey (T.C. 3935, dated 17 January 1942).

[Turkish Ambassador in] London to [Foreign Ministry in] Ankara, signed Aras: Turkish Ambassador's impressions and conclusions from interview with Eden on war situation (T.C. 3936, dated 20 January 1942).

[Turkish Ambassador in] London to [Foreign Ministry in] Ankara, signed Aras: Churchill's return to London [from a conference with Roosevelt ending on 14 January]. General expectations as to his statement (T.C. 3939, dated 21 January 1942).

[Turkish Ambassador in] Teheran to [Foreign Ministry in] Ankara, signed Soheily: situation in Persia, Russian encroachments (Iran.C. 743, dated 3 January 1942).

25 January 1942

[Persian Ambassador in] Ankara to [Persian Foreign Ministry in] Teheran: Persian Ambassador's conversation with Turkish Foreign Minister (Iran.C. 745, dated 9 January 1942).

Shortage of aviation spirit in Britain (——, No. 231,541, dated 22 January 1942).

Soviet Russian-Polish differences of opinion on nationality of various cities—Lemberg [Lvov] etc. (——, No. 231,653, dated 22 January 1942).

Polish view of coming developments in the Soviet Union (——, No. 231,661, dated 23 January 1942).

28 January 1942

French Embassy in Washington to Foreign Ministry in Vichy: [Senator Thomas] Connally's statement on Hongkong; Argentina's attitude at the Rio Conference (F.C. 17908, dated 22 January 1942).

2 February 1942

Remark of Mihai Antonescu on German-Rumanian relations (——, No. 232,647, dated 31 January 1942).

[Turkish] Foreign Ministry in Ankara to Turkish Ambassador in London: form of withdrawal of the Turkish Ambassador in London (T.C. 3977, dated 27 January 1942).

3 February 1942

Turkish Minister in Cairo to [Foreign Ministry in] Ankara: German counter-offensive in Libya and views of the British in Egypt thereon (T.C. 4020, dated 31 January 1942).

4 February 1942

Turkish Ambassador in London on [his] interview with [Soviet Ambassador] Maisky after the Moscow conferences (——, No. 232,790, dated 1 February 1942).

Finnish report from Tokyo, about Japanese military preparations on the Soviet frontier (——, No. 232,905, dated 2 February 1942).

7 February 1942

Turkish Ambassador in Kuibyshev to [Foreign Ministry in] Ankara: plans for Soviet attack round Smolensk (T.C. 4026, dated 4 February 1942).

8 February 1942

[Italian Ambassador in] Ankara to [Foreign Ministry in] Rome, signed de Peppo: Eden's visit to Moscow; Turkish-Russian relations. (It.C. 9898,9899, dated 30 January 1942).

[Bulgarian Minister in] Moscow to [Foreign Ministry in] Sofia: supply situation in Russia (B.C.239, dated 2 February 1942).

Bulgarian representative in Moscow to Sofia: worsening of morale in Moscow (B.C. 242, dated 5 February 1942).

[Foreign Office] London to Consul-General, Leopoldville: guidance on the week's news—Far East, Russia, Libya, Ireland. (E.C. 46, dated 5 February 1942).

French Governor-General in Indochina to Vichy: [Japanese] conquest of Malayan peninsula (F.C. 17976, dated 5 February 1942).

Situation in the Soviet Union (——, No. 233,334, dated 6 February 1942).

11 February 1942

[Italian Ambassador in] Tokyo to [Foreign Ministry in] Rome: future Japanese military operations (It.C. 9925, dated 6 February 1942).

[Turkish Ambassador in] Moscow to [Foreign Ministry in] Ankara: transfer of German [Army?] headquarters; Soviet operations towards Smolensk (T.C. 4053, dated 5 February 1942).

13 February 1942

Yugoslav Ambassador in Ankara to [Yugoslav] Foreign Ministry in London: Saracoglu's optimistic comment on Soviet collaboration with Balkan *bloc* (Jug.C. 1846, dated 10 February 1942).

15 February 1942

[Foreign Office] London to [Consul-General] Leopoldville: guidance on the [news from] the Pacific, Russia and Libya (E.C. 55, dated 12 February 1942).

16 February 1942

Foreign Ministry in Ankara to [Turkish] Ambassador in Berlin:

German–Soviet prisoner of war exchange (T.C. 4090, dated 13 February 1942).

British settlement of Egyptian government crisis (——, No. 234,265, dated 14 February 1942).

22 February 1942

[Foreign Office] London to [Consul-General in] Leopoldville: guidance on [the news from] the Pacific, the Eastern Front, and Japan (E.C. 70, dated 19 February 1942).

Egyptian Minister in Washington to [Egyptian] Foreign Ministry in Cairo: report on Bullitt's journey (Ag.C. 95, dated 9 February 1942).

Turkish Ambassador in London to [Foreign Ministry in] Ankara: Churchill's speech, morale of the British public, the India question (T.C. 4115, dated 17 February 1942).

20 February 1942

[French Minister in] Ottawa to Vichy: *Anschluss* of Canada to the U.S.A. (F.C. 18040, dated 14 February 1942).

[Italian Ambassador in] Santiago to [Foreign Ministry in] Rome: American concern over the war in the Far East, German U-boats in the Atlantic and trade with South America (It.C. 9993, dated 12 February 1942).

23 February 1942

[Foreign Office] London to Salisbury, Rhodesia: British air activities 8–15 February (E.C. 66, dated 17 February 1942).

[British Embassy in] Baghdad to [Foreign Office] London: effect of the loss of Singapore on the Irak population (E.C. 68, dated 18 February 1942).

24 February 1942

Turkish Ambassador in Vichy to Foreign Ministry in Ankara: Petain's question to Turkish Ambassador about Turkey (T.C. 4125, dated 8 January 1942).

Turkish diplomatic reports from Budapest about preparations for offensive (——, No. 235,155, dated 21 February 1942).

26 February 1942

Turkish Ambassador in London on his interview with Mr Churchill (——, No. 235,311, dated 23 February 1942).

1 March 1942

Yugoslav Minister in Moscow to [Yugoslav Foreign Ministry in] London: Russian supply situation (Jug.C. 1851, dated 21 February 1942).

[Portuguese Foreign Ministry in] Lisbon to Leopoldville: joint defence of South Africa, Angola and Belgian Congo (Port.C. 61, dated 22 February 1942).

[American Ambassador in] Kuibyshev to [State Department in] Washington: Stalin's Order of the Day on the occasion of Red Army Day (A.C. 9236, dated 24 February 1942).

Turkish attitude towards Germany and Great Britain (——, No. 235,560, dated 26 February 1942).

2 March 1942

[Italian Ambassador in] Ankara to [Foreign Ministry in] Rome: remark of the Turkish Ambassador in London to de Peppo (It.C. 10084, dated 25 February 1942).

[Italian Ambassador in] Kabul to [Foreign Ministry in] Rome: British plans for India (It.C. 10131, dated 27 February 1942).

3 March 1942

[Japanese Ambassador in] Kabul to [Foreign Ministry in] Tokyo: remarks of Jinnah and Gandhi (J.C. 6118, dated 28 February 1942).

2 March 1943

[French Minister in] Chungking to Vichy: consequences of Chiang Kai-Shek's journey to India (F.C. 18087, dated 25 February 1942).

4 March 1942

Rumours of imminent German operation against Sweden (——, No. 235,893, dated 2 March 1942).

5 March 1942

Defence of Portuguese colonies in Africa (Port.C. 69, dated 2 March 1942).

[Turkish Ambassador in] Kuibyshev to [Foreign Ministry in] Ankara: foodstuff difficulties, health and transportation in Russia (T.C. 4196, dated 3 March 1942).

[Turkish Foreign Ministry in] Ankara to [Turkish Ambassador in] Cairo: agreement between British and Saudi-Arabai (T.C. 4171, dated 27 February 1942).

[Turkish Ambassador in] Kuibyshev to [Foreign Ministry in] Ankara: activation of Tenth British Army in Iraq and Persia (T.C. 4164, dated 2 March 1942).

6 March 1942

[Rumanian Minister in] Vichy to [Foreign Ministry in] Bucharest: Pétain's comment on the situation on the occasion of an interview with Hiott (Rum.C. 797, dated 28 February 1942).

[Turkish Ambassador in] Stockholm to [Foreign Ministry in] Ankara: induction of recruits in Sweden; Duke of Coburg in Sweden, candidacy for Norwegian throne (T.C. 4175, dated 28 February 1942).

Stalin's alleged dissatisfaction with British foreign policy (——, No. 236,131, dated 3 March 1942).

[Turkish Ambassador in] Tokyo to [Foreign Ministry in] Ankara: change of Japanese Ambassador in Moscow (T.C. 4185, dated 3 March 1942).

[Turkish Ambassador in] Tokyo to [Foreign Ministry in] Ankara: Japanese troops sent to Manchuria (T.C. 4193, dated 4 March 1942).

[Italian Ambassador in] Kabul to [Foreign Ministry in] Rome: Nehru's comments on British government reshuffle (It.C. 10130, dated 4 March 1942).

9 March 1942

[Yugoslav Minister in] Ankara to [Yugoslav Foreign Ministry in] London: Yugoslav Minister's interview with Saracoglu on eventualities of the immediate future (Jug.C. 1856, dated 27 February 1942).

[Turkish Ambassador in] Kuibyshev to [Foreign Ministry in] Ankara: row over the establishment of an Allied second front in Europe (T.C. 4200, dated 3 March 1942).

[Foreign Office in] London to [Consul-General in] Leopoldville: guidance [on the news on] the Pacific, France, Russia, U.S.A. (E.C. 97, dated 5 March 1942).

Yugoslav report from Kuibyshev: verbal statement of Soviet [Foreign] Commissar on the political and military situation (——, No. 236,511, dated 7 March 1942).

Anxiety of the Union of South Africa about Madagascar (——, No. 236,530, dated 7 March 1942).

[A British plan to occupy Madagascar had been under consideration since December 1941; the island was occupied by force during May 1942).

Japanese Foreign Minister on petroleum supplies to Japan (——, No. 236,543, dated 7 March 1942).

10 March 1942

[Turkish Ambassador in] Moscow to [Foreign Ministry in] Ankara: fighting around Rzhev and Staraya Russya (T.C. 4205, dated 2 March 1942).

[Turkish Ambassador in] Kuibyshev to [Foreign Ministry in] Ankara: journey of Soviet Ambassador to Tokyo, to Kuibyshev; recall of Japanese Ambassador to Kuibyshev (T.C. 4206, dated 3 March 1943).

[Italian Ambassador in] Tokyo to [Foreign Ministry in] Rome: remark of Sato about a Moscow Mission (It.C. 10143, dated 7 March 1942).

[Italian Ambassador in] Kabul to [Foreign Ministry in] Rome: British countermeasures to put down the resistance in the Indian people (It.C. 10157, dated 7 March 1942).

[American Embassy in] Ankara to [State Department in] Washington: American Ambassador Steinhardt's conversation with Soviet Ambassador about conjectural Axis plans against Turkey (A.C. 9268, dated 7 March 1942).

11 March 1942

[Yugoslav Minister in] Ankara to [Yugoslav Foreign Ministry in] London: Saracoglu fears German pressure on Turkey after the Eastern Offensive (Jug.C. 1856a, dated 27 February 1942).

12 March 1942

Situation in Serbia and Slovenia (——, No. 236,662, dated 9 March 1942).

[Italian Minister in] Helsinki to [Foreign Ministry in] Rome: American threats against Finland (It.C. 10158, dated 9 March 1942).

14 March 1942

[French Ambassador in] Washington to Vichy: exchange of views between [French Ambassador] Henry-Haye and [Under-Secretary of State] Sumner Welles about the [R.A.F.] air raid on Paris. (F.C. 18130, dated 6 March 1942). [During an R.A.F. air raid on Paris on 3/4 March 1942, over 800 Parisians had been killed.]

[Turkish Ambassador in] Moscow to [Foreign Ministry in] Ankara: [German] air raid on Moscow, 5/6 March (T.C. 4224, dated 7 March 1942).

[Turkish Ambassador in London] to [Foreign Ministry in] Ankara: British-American-Russian agreement on postwar problems (T.C. 4223, dated 8 March 1942).

[Foreign Ministry in] Ankara to [Turkish Minister in] Stockholm: Swedish mediation in the conclusion of a German-Russian armistice (T.C. 4226, dated 10 March 1942).

[Turkish Ambassador in] Kuibyshev to [Foreign Ministry in] Ankara: Turkish Military Attache's interview with Foreign relations division of National Defence Commissariat (T.C. 4228, dated 28 February 1942).

[Turkish Ambassador in] Tokyo to [Foreign Ministry in] Ankara: effect of Japanese successes in China (T.C. 4237, dated 11 March 1942).

Report of Portuguese Minister in Ankara: Turkish foreign policy (——, No. 236,915, dated 11 March 1942).

Report of Italian Minister in Kabul: situation in India (——, No. 236,931 dated 11 March 1942).

Turkish report on the situation in Moscow on Red Army Day (——, No. 237,028, dated 12 March 1942).

15 March 1942

[Yugoslav Minister in] Kuibyshev to [Yugoslav Foreign Ministry in] London: remarks of Turkish Ambassador in Kuibyshev on the possibility of peace between Germany and Russia (Jug.C. 1859, dated 12 March 1942).

[Turkish Ambassador in] Kuibyshev to [Foreign Ministry in] Ankara: differences of opinion between Russia and Britain on account of Second Front (T.C. 4251, dated 12 March 1942).

19 March 1942

[Italian Minister in] Kabul to [Foreign Ministry in] Rome: situation in India (It.C. 10191, dated 12 March 1942).

21 March 1942

Yugoslav report: American Ambassador Steinhardt on U.S.A.s resolve to fight on until final victory (——, No. 237,880, dated 19 March 1942).

22 March 1942

[Turkish Ambassador in] Kuibyshev to [Foreign Ministry in] Ankara: Russia's demand to Britain; necessary for Churchill to go to Moscow (T.C. 4268, dated 16 March 1942).

24 March 1942

[American Ambassador in] Teheran to [State Department] Washington: Axis propaganda in Persia (A.C. 9282, dated 18 March 1942).

25 March 1942

[Foreign Office in] London to [Consul-General in] Leopoldville: guidance [on the news from] the Far East, Russia, Persia (E.C. 117, dated 17 March 1942).

[Japanese Minister in] Helsinki to [Foreign Ministry in] Tokyo: food supply difficulties in Soviet Russia (Jap.C. 6173, dated 19 March 1942).

[Summary report] on the Situation in Persia (——, No. 238,087, dated 20 March 1942).

American Minister in Cairo to [American] Embassy in London: German plans and preparations in the Middle East (A.C. 9275, dated 13 March 1942).

[State Department in] Washington to [American Ambassador in] in Kuibyshev: United States fears exploitation of assassination attempt on von Papen for anti-Allied propaganda in Turkey. The Hungarian contribution to the Spring Offensive. (A.C. 9276, dated 14 March 1942). [A bomb had been thrown at the German Ambassador in Turkey, von Papen, without injuring him; the Turkish government had begun an inquiry, but fearing diplomatic repercussions proceeded only dilatorily when clear evidence of the Soviet inspiration of the attempt was found. The Germans did not in the event make much propaganda out of it, as they had good cause to keep the word 'assassination' out of the public usage as much as possible.—The unpublished fragments of the *Goebbels Diaries* show this tendency well.]

[Turkish Ambassador in] Kuibyshev to [Foreign Ministry in] Ankara: strength of the Russian Army; Polish General Anders' complaints to Stalin (T.C. 4277, dated 17 March 1942).

27 March 1942

[Turkish representative] Lagos to [Foreign Ministry in] Ankara: interview of Turkish Ambassador Orbay with Cripps on Russia and the general situation (T.C. 4279, dated 17 March 1942).

[Turkish Ambassador in Kuibyshev to Foreign Ministry in Ankara?] Arming of only three Polish divisions by the Russians (T.C. 4295, dated 21 March 1942).

[Turkish Ambassador in] Kuibyshev to [Foreign Ministry in] Ankara: situation in Leningrad (TC.. 4297, dated 23 March 1942).

28 March 1942

British justification for restriction of war material supplies to Turkey (——, No. 238,415, dated 25 March 1942).

Report of Turkish chargé d'affaires in Teheran (——, No. 238,501, dated 25 March 1942).

[Turkish Ambassador in] Kuibyshev to [Foreign Ministry in] Ankara: replacement of Australian and New Zealand troops in Egypt and Syria with Poles from Russia (T.C. 4305, dated 24 March 1942).

30 March 1942

[Foreign Ministry in] Rome to [Italian Ambassador in] Bucharest: Ciano's visit to Bucharest (It.C. 10305, dated 26 March 1942).

31 March 1942

[Turkish Ambassador in] Kuibyshev to [Foreign Ministry in] Ankara: living conditions in Kuibyshev (T.C. 4314, dated 26 March 1942).

[State Department in] Washington to [Foreign Ministry in] Vichy: Roosevelt would respond to a return by Laval to the government by breaking off diplomatic relations (A.C. 9285, dated 27 March 1942). [Pierre Laval was reappointed to the Government as Prime Minister, Foreign and Interior Minister on 18 April; the U.S. Ambassador, Admiral Leahy, who had been recalled to Washington for consultation of the previous day, did not return to Vichy and was not replaced.]

2 April 1942

[Italian Minister in] Kabul to [Foreign Ministry in] Rome: effect of Bose's propaganda on India (It.C. 10310, dated 24 March 1942). [Subbhas Chandra Bose, who had been a revolutionary youth movement leader in the inter-war period, was an Indian Nationalist leader subservient to the Axis].

[Italian Ambassador in] Tokyo to [Foreign Ministry in] Rome: Air link between Japan and Italy (It.C. 10398, dated 31 March 1942).

3 April 1942

[Turkish Ambassador in] London to [Foreign Ministry in] Ankara: Turkish Ambassador presents his credentials to Eden (T.C. 4319, dated 26 March 1942).

4 April 1942

[French Minister in] Lisbon to [Foreign Ministry in] Vichy: conversation between Finnish chargè d'affaires and [French] Minister: Finland cannot hold out in this war for one more winter (F.C. 18302, dated 1 April 1942).

6 April 1942

[Italian Minister in] Dublin to [Italian Legation in] Berne: depressed morale in Britain (It.C. 10361 dated 24 March 1942).

[Turkish Foreign Ministry in] Ankara to [Turkish Ambassador in] London: general problems, the American-British-Russian agreement on the New Order in Europe (T.C. 4328, dated 28 March 1942).

[Turkish Ambassador in] Kuibyshev to [Foreign Ministry in] Ankara: British and American supplies to Russia (T.C. 4324, dated 30 March 1942).

Diplomatic and military situation of the Allies in the Middle East (——, No. 239,406, dated 2 April 1942).

Bulgarian diplomatic report from Kuibyshev on the Winter Offensive (——, No. 239,454, dated 4 April 1942).

The Situation in China (——, No. 239,528, dated 4 April 1942).

[Turkish Ambassador in] Berlin to [Foreign Ministry in] Ankara: King Boris' visit to the Führer (T.C. 4342, dated 30 March 1942). [The visit took place on 24 March 1942].

[Turkish Foreign Ministry in] Ankara to [Turkish Ambassador in] London: two interviews of the Turkish Foreign Minister with British Ambassador (T.C. 4339, dated 31 March 1942).

6 April 1942

Polish Foreign Ministry in London to [Polish] Ambassador in —— [sic]: Polish Memorandum on the future frontiers in Europe (P.C. 848, dated 2 April 1942).

8 April 1942

[Swiss Minister in] Washington to [Foreign Ministry in] Berne:

German spring offensive in Russia (Schw.C. 2371, dated 1 April 1942).
[Italian Minister in] Lisbon to [Foreign Ministry in] Rome: lack of understanding among de Gaullists in England (It.C. 10384, dated 2 April 1942).

9 April 1942

The Situation in India (——, No. 239,540, dated 7 April 1942).
Yugoslav report from Kuibyshev about conjectures as to German spring offensive (——, No. 239,457, dated 4 April 1942).

10 April 1942

Apparent statement of Japanese chargé d'affaires in Kuibyshev on subject of objectives of the German spring offensive against the Soviet Union (——, No. 239,782, dated 9 April 1942; entry endorsed 'Note for Reich Foreign Minister'].
Supply of foodstuffs to the Red Army (——, No. 239,572, dated 7 April 1942).
Food supplies to the Red Army (——, No. 239,572, dated 7 April 1942).
Polish report from Kuibyshev on famine threatening the Soviet Union (——, No. 239,656, dated 7 April 1942).
Turkish diplomatic report from Budapest on the spring offensive (——, No. 239,714, dated 8 April 1942).
[Turkish Ambassador in] Moscow to [Foreign Ministry in] Ankara: situation in Moscow (T.C. 4374, dated 6 April 1942).
[French Ambassador in] Washington to [Foreign Ministry in] Vichy: unrest in China on account of Anglo-Indian talks (F.C. 18335, dated 7 April 1942).

11 April 1942

[Turkish Ambassador in] Kuibyshev to [Foreign Ministry in] Ankara: [German] air raid on Novorossiisk (T.C. 4359, dated 6 April 1942).

12 April 1942

[Turkish Ambassador in] Kuibyshev to [Foreign Ministry in] Ankara: arrival of American tanks and aircraft in Russia (T.C. 4369, dated 6 April 1942).
[American Minister in] Cairo to [American Embassy in] London: American call for air force units for Egypt (A.C. 9298, dated 31 March 1942).

[Turkish Foreign Ministry in] Ankara to [Turkish Ambassador in] London: Japan's advance on Australia, India, Russia (T.C. 4344, dated 3 April 1942).

[Turkish Minister in] Teheran to [Foreign Ministry in] Ankara: Polish General Anders' interview with Stalin (T.C. 4357, dated 6 April 1942).

Yugoslav report from Kuibyshev on German spring offensive (——, No. 239,715, dated 8 April 1942).

Turkish report from Tokyo on alleged postponement of German offensive (——, No. 239,972, dated 10 April 1942).

14 April 1942

[Turkish Foreign Ministry in] Ankara to [Turkish Ambassador in] Kuibyshev: British anxiety about Japanese victories: Spain's attitude (T.C. 4386, dated 9 April 1942).

15 April 1942

[Turkish Ambassador in] Kuibyshev to [Foreign Ministry in] Ankara: cut in food rations for diplomatic corps (T.C. 4384, dated 10 April 1942).

[Turkish Ambassador in] Kuibyshev to [Foreign Ministry in] Ankara: Russian aircraft production (T.C. 4389, dated 9 April 1942).

Swiss Minister in London to [Foreign Ministry in] Berne: British-Russian treaty of alliance (Schw.C. 2383, dated 9 April 1942). [On 8 April, the British Foreign Secretary suggested to the Russian Ambassador in London that negotiations for an Anglo-Russian Treaty should take place in London; M. Molotov, the Soviet Foreign Commissar, arrived in London on 20 May after protracted negotiations, and the treaty was signed on 26 May 1942].

United States Press on the Allied position (——, No. 240,173, dated 13 April 1942).

[Turkish Ambassador in Moscow] Haidar Aktai on an interview between [Sir Archibald] Clark Kerr [the new British Ambassador in Moscow] and Stalin on 28 March (——, No. 240, 175, dated 13 April 1942).

Developments in Soviet-Japanese relations (——, No. 240,199, dated 13 April 1942).

[Turkish Foreign Ministry in] Ankara to [Turkish Minister in] Cairo: visit of Turkish officers to the Libyan front (T.C. 4385, dated 8 April 1942).

[American Embassy in] Vichy to [State Department in] Washington, signed [Admiral] Leahy: conversation with Secretary-General for French North Africa (A.C. 9203, dated 5 April 1942).

Imminent journey by Haidar Aktai [Turkish Ambassador in Moscow] to Ankara (——, No. 240,260, dated 13 April 1942).

'On the Attempted Assassination of von Papen' (——, No. 240,274, dated 13 April 1942).

17 April 1942

[Yugoslav Minister in] Ankara to [Yugoslav Foreign Ministry in] London: will Germany attack Turkey? Turkey's admission of unconditional friendship towards Britain (Jug.C. 1909, dated 7 April 1942).

[Italian Foreign Ministry in] Rome to [Ambassador in] Tokyo: statement of Oshima on exploitation of captured raw materials (It.C. 10447, dated 13 April 1942).

[Turkish Ambassador in] Kuibyshev to [Foreign Ministry in] Ankara: Turkish Ambassador's journey from Kuibyshev to Ankara (T.C. 4401, dated 13 April 1941).

19 April 1942

[Turkish Foreign Ministry in] Ankara to [Turkish Ambassador in] Washington: Eden's conversation with Rauf Orbai on the Far East and Anglo-Soviet negotiations (T.C. 4417, dated 14 April 1942).

II

[The following passages have been excerpted from the War Diary of the German Naval Staff for the first two years of the war.]

5 September 1939
As on preceding days our Monitoring Service reports the rendezvous positions and routing directions broadcast by the British Admiralty to incoming ships in the Atlantic south-west of Britain and Ireland. (Forwarded to Atlantic U-boats.)

10 September 1939
British aircraft shot down on 4 September is raised. British *Faut* salvaged, and with its help the Monitoring Service fixes the positions of *Ark Royal*, *Nelson* and *Sheffield* (Home Fleet) near Dundee on 10 September.

15 February 1940
Supply ship *Altmark* proceeding southwards through Norwegian territorial waters. Ship has been located by the enemy. According to our radio monitoring, the British Admiralty warns Naval Commands, particularly the cruiser *Glasgow* and submarines *Seal*, *Triad* and *Orzil*, that according to a report from Tromsö a large German tanker of some 10,000 tons, painted black, passed by off Tromsö at 1215 hrs on 12 February.

16 February 1940
In view of the enemy activities intercepted by our Monitoring Service and the report from the supply ship *Altmark* Group West and the Naval Staff agree that the enemy will use every means—and has already taken extensive steps with his naval forces—to catch the *Altmark*. Our

previous assumption of the complete safety of the Norwegian territorial waters can not be supported any longer under these circumstances.

17 February 1940

W-T message from Commander-in-Chief in *Arethusa* (the W-T is available to us decoded at 0600 hrs). The C.-in-C. reports in this, that the destroyer *Cossack* is lying alongside *Altmark* and he is returning with his group to Rosyth. There were no German prisoners in *Arethusa*. The submarine *Seal* is going to wait for a time outside Jössing Fjord.

13 March 1940

[A decoded Admiralty order places British destroyer units under the Commander-in-Chief of the Home Fleet.] This reinforcement of the destroyer strength of the Home Fleet is particularly remarkable when considered in conjunction with the other measures of the British naval forces and the Home Fleet's concentration at Scapa.

In addition to this information, our radio reconnaissance again succeeds in intercepting details of the new deployment of the British submarines, by decoding signals, and comes thereby to an exceptionally important and significant conclusion: contrary to the previous distribution of submarines in the North Sea, there are on 13 March altogether *fifteen British submarines*, that is twice to three times as many submarines as previously, lying in wait off the Skagerrak. . . .(1) Either this is flank protection for a major landing operation planned by the enemy in Norway; . . . [or] (2) the enemy has learned of some of the preparations on the German side, and fears a German operation against Norwegian territory.

15 March 1940

Our radio reconnaissance intercepts two very important items. . . . (1) The British submarine deployment in the North Sea off the Skagerrak and the German Bight is being dispersed. . . . From this information we can conclude that in consequence of the unexpected Finnish peace, the planned operation [of the British against Norway] has been *postponed*. (2) Our decoding service has also succeeding in partially decoding an order issued by the Admiralty at 1437 hrs on 14 March to the Commander-in-Chief, Home Fleet, [etc.] re: 'Plan 3', from which the following is extracted: (*a*) preparations for troop embarkations on a major scale have been put in hand and are complete: . . . (*b*) the troop transports receive new sailing alerts (48 hours, 96 hours, 80 hours), presumably as a provisional order until the political situation is clarified. . . . There is *nothing* in the signals which indicates a complete *cancellation* of the Norway operation, whose basic planning can no longer be a matter of doubt.

23 March 1940

The main British radio cipher system has changed its code on 22 March. We must reckon with ten to fourteen days during which our radio monitoring service cannot read them.

30 March 1940

The Rumanian Minister in Oslo reports to his Foreign Ministry [in Bucharest]: it has made a strong impression in Norway that France and Britain may alter their attitude towards Norway. He has gained the impression from a conversation with the British Minister [in Oslo] that no far-reaching decisions have been reached in London and Paris about respecting Norwegian territorial waters for the time being, particularly since Norway herself seems determined to prevent Germany's using the Norwegian territorial waters, in order to avoid grave British counter-measures.

1 April 1940

The Swiss Minister in Stockholm reports to his Government: German and British troop-landings on the Norwegian coast are imminent!!

5 April 1940

Radio monitoring service intercepted a British W-T signal, in which orders are given for submarine operations. On account of lack of decoding possibilities, only the position of one submarine, *Triton*, at 57° . . ., 10° . . . East could be hinted at. From the length of the signal (188 groups) the Monitoring Service considers it safe to assume that these are orders for the operations of fifteen to twenty submarines. It is possible that some of them have been ordered to undertake special operation 'D'.

7 April 1940

Our telephone interception service intercepted telephone conversations between the Danish naval attaché [in Berlin] and the Danish and Norwegian Ministers, in which he asked for an immediate interview, as he had information of the utmost political importance and bearing to convey to them. It is possible that the Danish naval attaché has received knowledge of the coming operation *Weserübung* [the German invasion of Norway]!!

20 April 1940
The Turkish Ambassador reports from Rome: 'Count Ciano is said to have stated that after the occupation of Albania by Italy, Corfu has no longer any importance for the defence of the Adriatic. For Italy it is therefore pointless to undertake adventures in the form of an occupation of Corfu.'

The Yugoslav Foreign Minister reports to his Legation in Berlin: 'The British Blockade Minister has stated in London that Britain does not want a war in the South-East [of Europe]. Britain believed that Germany also wanted to avoid this.'

27 April 1940
As the enemy has again partially changed his codes on 26 April our insight into the enemy's wireless traffic is at present seriously impeded.

27 May 1940
Our radio monitoring service has intercepted a very valuable wireless signal, which gives a clear picture of the make-up of the Northern Patrol south of Iceland. The auxiliary cruisers *Forfar, Andania, Wolfe* and an unknown one received a line of position of 160° from Stokkanes (Iceland), at distances of 25, 50, 75 and 100 sea miles. Commencing on 21 May, 2100 hrs, the ships are to patrol tracks of 245° and 65°, doubling back after every twelve hours (after six hours on the first occasion.) *Southampton* is informed of this order, and can thus be presumed to be in the Northern Patrol. As the last such order was in force for 28 days, we can also assume that this one will be valid for some time. This gives us exceptional chances for our battleships to operate out of Trondheim.

22 June 1940
According to despatches by foreign diplomats, differences of opinion have emerged in the British Cabinet on whether to continue the prosecution of the war. Some of its Members are apparently in favour of negotiations with Germany. From a telegram of the *Italian* Minister in

Sweden to Rome it emerges that the British Minister in Stockholm has told Foreign Minister Günther that Britain is ready to enter into peace talks with Germany and Italy. A report of similar content has arrived from Hungary; the report must provisionally be viewed with great reserve.

4 August 1940

In consequence of the change of various British codes, insight into British radio traffic is impeded at present and will be for the next two to three weeks.

21 August 1940

On 20 August, simultaneous changeover by all codes and ciphers of the British Navy systems! Thus it is no longer possible to reckon with results from decoding for the time being. This fact is the heaviest blow to our radio monitoring since the beginning of the war. The enemy has maintained the same codes since long before the war, and has hitherto just caused our decoding service temporary difficulties by cipher changes introduced from time to time. The activities of our radio monitoring and decoding services were considerably facilitated by the capture of quantities of enemy documents, so that in parts we had nearly complete knowledge of the enemy's radio traffic. It was to be expected that the enemy would sooner or later carry out a basic change in his coding system, to re-establish his wireless security; and in this connection it is a remarkable fact that he has taken this step only now, a year after war has broken out. We cannot count on the monitoring service's being in the position to deliver new information for at least six weeks, after first cracking the new wireless procedures of the enemy.

9 September 1940

Foreign Ambassadors in Moscow are reporting an increasing tension in the relationship between Germany and Russia. The Vienna Award which was announced without Russia's participation, is said to have caused strong misgivings in Moscow circles. There is concern and confusion about the objectives of Germany's Eastern Policies (and policies in Poland).

22 November 1940

Radio monitoring intercepts a British Army wireless message, from which emerge unambiguously certain preparations for an imminent military operation against Ireland (see Monitoring Report 1540). The High Command and Foreign Ministry have been informed.

24 November 1940
Political information reinforces the impression gained from radio interception of an imminent operation by Britain against Ireland. The British side are using allegations of a planned German occupation of Ireland to justify this. [Hitler had long before rejected such an operation, when suggested to him by the Naval Staff.]

25 November 1940
De Valera announces on 23 November again that he will do everything to prevent Ireland's being drawn into the war. The British could *not* fear a German invasion of Ireland.

1 December 1940
[There is a lengthy report in the section on 'Our Sea Transport', in which reports intercepted by the German radio monitoring service are reproduced, clearly proving that America is acting against Germany in the Atlantic.]

4 January 1941
On 3 January (evening) the Admiralty instructed all merchant ships to deliver up their envelopes with the code tables for the Merchant Navy Code, reference S.P. 02272 (8) and S.P. 02272 (9) at their next port, to the Naval Control Service Officer. These are the codes captured by our Ship 16, which were just due to come into force. The value of this captured material is thus regrettably lost for our decoding service.

19 February 1941
Antonescu has informed the Turkish Ambassador (in Bucharest) that Rumania, as Germany's ally, can no longer supply Turkey with fuels. The Turkish Minister stated that Turkey would only enter the war if her own borders were attacked.

17 March 1941
The Chief of the 2nd department, Naval Staff, reports that we have succeeded in cracking the Merchant Naval Code.

4 April 1941

The Chief of Naval Operations reports that the American Navy, which has hitherto used a very simple code system, has changed it and brought into service a new and at present uncrackable coding procedure. Our decoding service, which has been able up to the present to decipher the American system without difficulties, is confronted with a grave problem and has lost its insight. There are also very important changes detectable in the Russian wireless traffic. For two days running new wireless and coding systems were employed, evidently as a preparation for mobilisation. After two days, they reverted to the old systems.

22 April 1941

The British Minister in Ankara forwarded to the Foreign Office in London on 14 April, as we learn from a decoded wireless message, an agent's report that Germany will scarcely turn against Turkey in the foreseeable future, as Russia's attitude would be dubious in such an event. Germany wants no conflict with Russia, as in an advance into the Russian expanses Germany would have to fear for the voids left behind her front lines. Germany would be forced, by the retreat of every government official in the wake of the Russian armies to reorganise the entire country from the bottom up (see Monitoring Report 1430).

24 April 1941

According to a statement by the Italian Counsellor of Embassy [in Moscow], the British Ambassador Cripps has predicted that the war on Russia will begin on 22 June!! In foreign diplomats' circles the prediction is otherwise 20 May!

1 May 1940

[Several of the signals of the British naval attaché in Stockholm were intercepted during March to May 1941]. Of some significance is a report from the British naval attaché in Stockholm to the Admiralty on 26 April, that according to a neutral captain Kristiansand was 'full of German sea transport' on about 16 April, and that there was very noticeable activity in the military transports, in which among others tanks of vehicles could be seen.

6 June 1941

The American Ambassador [Admiral] Leahy has called on Marshal

Pétain with a special mission from President Roosevelt, to ask for precise information on future French policy towards Britain and Germany and the results of the last two Cabinet sittings. The American Government is evidently gravely concerned about the way things are going. The French Embassy in Washington has been given an urgent warning *not* to consider the far-reaching German demands. Hull has stated that should the German demands be fulfilled, France would be militarily and politically entirely subservient to Germany, and would thus constitute 'a tool of aggression'. He has hinted perceptibly that in such an event America would seize the French possessions in the Western Hemisphere.

20 July 1941

According to our radio monitoring service, wireless messages were heard in the British 'line' traffic [two-station radio communication on one or two frequencies] between Reykjavik and Horsea, from the America radio station N3X (probably the U.S. Naval Commander, Iceland) to the Chief of U.S. Naval Operations. In the British address, in addition to unidentified addressee-groups, there is also the British Admiralty! From this it can be deduced that the Royal Navy is provided *with American code devices!*

III

DECODED MATERIAL SHOWN
TO DR JOSEPH GOEBBELS

7 February 1942

We have come into possession of a secret directive sent out by the Foreign Office to British embassies and legations abroad. In this, the British Foreign Office warns against undue optimism over the situation on the Eastern Front. The German Army has not been defeated by any means, it says, but is displaying an unbroken power of resistance; one must presume that as soon as the weather improves, it will go over to new offensive operations.*

6 April 1942

I have been given an analysis of trends in British propaganda since the beginning of the war, prepared by the *Forschungsamt*. It yields little information that is basically new. Beyond all doubt, British propaganda has failed abysmally in this war. It has no uniform objectives, its slogans are changed from one instance to the next, and thus it lacks real punch. All you can learn from it is how not to do things.

28 April 1942

Ministerial-Counsellor Seifert and the *Forschungsamt's* liaison officer Severith called to brief me on the work of the *Forschungsamt*. This is very extensive, employs all the most modern technical equipment and extracts all manner of unusual secret material from the enemy's communication services. Above all they have succeeded in breaking most of the enemy's codes so that it is today possible for us to monitor part of the telegraphic traffic between Ankara and London or between London and Moscow. I am to receive the results of this work regularly

---

* [These are extracts from the original typescript of the diaries kept by the Propaganda Minister Dr Goebbels, who was a recipient of some of the *Forschungsamt's* reports and summaries. The diaries, largely unpublished, are held by the National Archives in Washington and by the Institut für Zeitgeschichte in Munich.]

in future. It will be possible to draw a whole series of important conclusions from them. Of course, this work must be kept extremely secret
as its effectiveness would be wasted otherwise. By the way, British
methods in this field are extraordinarily careless. I only hope that this
is not the case with our own secret communications as well; for if the
British knew in detail about us everything that we know about them
it could have very grave consequences.

11 May 1942

Severith, my liaison officer to the *Forschungsamt*, has brought me a few
confidential reports: the Japanese embassy in Moscow is undertaking
attempts designed to bring about a separate peace between Germany
and the Soviet Union. We have learned this from telegrams we have
intercepted and decoded. The Japanese seem to have no particular desire
to intervene in the German-Russian conflict at present as they are too
heavily engaged elsewhere. But I consider their attempts pointless. We
will not have peace with the Soviet Union until she is beaten.

16 May 1942

I have received from the *Forschungsamt* material on a series of political
matters which are of some interest. Relations between Turkey and the
Soviet Union have become exceptionally acrimonious. In private conversations the Turkish Foreign Minister Saracoglu is using the most
virulent language against the Soviet Union's foreign policy. The G.P.U.
[Soviet secret service] is trying to interfere in internal Turkish affairs
and has achieved masterpieces of distortion of truth in the trial of those
behind the assassination attempt on von Papen. Even so, I do not expect
much from this development at present. Ankara will doubtless wait and
see how things go militarily during the coming summer, before defining
her future attitude.

Work is proceeding blithely on the Stalin-Eden plan. Stalin is
demanding from the British the restitution of Russia's pre-war [i.e.
pre-1941] frontiers, plus the Baltic States, part of Finland and much of
South-East Europe. And in their plight, the British are even prepared
to make these concessions to the Bolsheviks. But the secret sources
show that the United States are showing extreme reservations about
such a procedure. Fear of the Soviets is also very pronounced in Conservative circles in London. Of course they want the Russians to destroy
Germany, but then again they do not want them to make any gains in

Continental Europe. What they have been trying to forbid Germany, namely leadership in Europe, they certainly do not want to hand over to the Soviets. All these problems are still only at the stage of vague discussion. The British will doubtless agree to make any concessions to Stalin once the water is up to their necks.

30 May 1942

A secret report put together by the *Forschungsamt* for me shows that very intensive negotiations are in hand between Moscow and London on the shape of post-war Europe. Among other things, M. Molotov is said to have been in London for some days already, to put his signature to a treaty to this effect. All these rumours cannot be checked at present, however. From the *Forschungsamt's* secret report one can see that the British are very much more accommodating to the Bolsheviks than the Americans are. In their predicament they are ready to grant the Russians everything they ask for. Above all they would permit them to swallow up all the small border states without further ado, quite apart from Germany which the British would just love to see destroyed and decimated. The United States are offering major resistance to this. They are endeavouring to keep so far from these negotiations, as it is quite easy to see, that the fear of Bolshevism which has almost completely vanished in Britain still seems to lurk in the Americans' hearts.

25 September 1942

The head of the *Forschungsamt*, Ministerial-Direktor Seifert, briefed me on the monitoring and 'research' (i.e. intercepting and decrypting) methods employed by the *Forschungsamt*. They are very extensive and necessitate a major organisation. But the results make the effort worthwhile. Seifert would like me to let him have certain kinds of corrections to the intercept materials supplied to me, but I rejected this request. The *Forschungsamt* should work with absolutely no preconceived notions, even though false interpretations and errors may from time to time be the result. If one is to give the *Forschungsamt* instructions, it will try to 'research' within the framework of these instructions; that is to say, it will then be biassed and will undoubtedly yield fewer results than at present under its freelance 'research' activity. The main thing is for the *Forschungsamt*, along with the many other agencies investigating and evaluating the international situation, to provide us with the best picture of political and diplomatic cross-currents that can be sifted from the intercepted despatches. If the *Forschungsamt* were to be asked to follow certain tendencies, then it will become just that: tendentious, and its reports will forfeit their value for the formation of judgments.

8 December 1942

I am reading a detailed memorandum put together by the *Forschungsamt* on the Darlan case, in which this French admiral's treachery is depicted from its earliest beginnings. It proves quite clearly that Darlan hightailed it to North Africa just for the purpose of defecting, and that his son's illness was only a cover for this. One can even read into the documents possible evidence that Pétain was hand in glove with him; but this is only supposition, which cannot be proved. Be it as it may, the French are paying dearly for their treason. They have lost their Mother Country, they have lost their fleet, and they have lost their Colonies.

14 February 1943

Apart from this, I have learned from reports of the *Forschungsamt* that at the Adana conference Churchill has proposed a three-way partition of Europe—into Southern, Northern and Central blocs. Churchill has put it to the Turks that he has no intention of destroying the German Reich. But of course one knows just how much to believe of these Churchillian protestations.

16 February 1943

Confidential reports of the *Forschungsamt* disclose that the Japanese Ambassador in Kuibyshev, Sato, who has of course already been conspicuous for his unpleasant remarks about us, has even partially condemned Axis policies and military strategy. He is said to be suffering from a liver-complaint, and this is why he views the situation rather pessimistically. He suspects that once the Soviets have attained worthwhile successes on their western front they will undertake a campaign against Japan. That in my opinion is the very last thing the Kremlin is thinking of at present.

Our propaganda against Moscow is having an exceptionally strong effect as I can see from these confidential monitoring reports. Public opinion in Spain has been deeply inflamed. The belief there is that Britain has neither the desire nor the ability to do anything tangible against the Bolshevism gaining ground at home. Spain is certainly not hopeful of any salvation from that quarter.

18 February 1943

[The aftermath of Goebbels' famous 'total war' speech in the Sport-palast in Berlin.] They said that one could call it a real fighting speech, the like of which has not been heard since the days of our accession to power. That is the verdict of the majority of the foreign journalists. As I can see from the telephone conversations monitored by the *Forschungsamt* this impression voiced by the journalists who attended the demonstration in the Sportpalast is absolutely genuine. They discuss it among themselves in private conversation in just the same terms as they have used in their commentaries.

20 February 1943

Confidential reports of the *Forschungsamt* indicate to me that the Diplomatic Corps at Kuibyshev is exceptionally disconcerted [by the German defeat at Stalingrad]. They still hope that the German resistance will suffice to bring the Soviet steamroller to a halt. While up to now they have been hoping by and large for a Bolshevik victory, now they seem to have got cold feet. The Bolshevik successes have horrified and above all bewildered them all. Stalin is also treating the Anglo-Saxon diplomats very rudely: he feels sure he is master of the situation.

21 February 1943

As I can see from the *Forschungsamt*'s reports, Churchill is taking great pains to normalise Turco-Soviet relations one way or another. But the Turks are becoming very suspicious. There can be no talk whatsoever of Churchill having succeeded in overcoming these Turkish suspicions. People are contemplating the Soviet victories with one eye weeping and one smiling. In any event they are absolutely clear that if Bolshevism were to overrun the Reich it would very soon be all over with Turkey's national independence.

11 March 1943

The Times deeply regrets the pronounced effectiveness of the anti-Bolshevik propaganda I have initiated and states that if it continues as it has up to now, the rift in the enemy camp will become irreparable. The British Foreign Office associates itself wholeheartedly with *The Times*' arguments and sends a directive to its Press Attachés that they are to combat the anti-Bolshevik propaganda of the Axis Powers wherever possible, and with every means at their disposal.

. . . A study by the *Forschungsamt* is shown to me containing a despatch by the Turkish Ambassador in the United States. This despatch is packed with anxieties and worries about the growth of Bolshevism, not only in the military but also in the propaganda and political fields. One can see from this despatch that the Soviet appetite has caused the greatest consternation in Turkey. At any rate, it is now clear to me that our greatest chances now lie in pursuing anti-Bolshevik propaganda.

13 March 1943

. . . In this connection a speech by the former Ambassador Bullitt is interesting; in it, he quite openly warns the Soviets that it will be necessary to dangle a carrot in front of them and beat them from behind with a stick, like a donkey. . . . A lengthy report from the *Forschungsamt* investigates this same line; mistrust of Moscow in the whole enemy camp, nourished very largely by the neutral countries. Above all Ankara is outspoken on this. The Turks are of course the next ones to be swallowed by the Russian bear, if the German forces should not be in the position to knock out its teeth first of all.

17 April 1943

I have received from the *Forschungsamt* secret information supporting the belief that Roosevelt is planning to meet Stalin somewhere. It must be said that this information is still quite unsubstantiated. At any rate I can see from the statements of the diplomats that there has been an element of *rapprochement* between the Soviet and the American points of view. So Eden's visit to the United States appears not to have passed quite so unsuccessfully as we had earlier assumed.

18 April 1943

From a secret *Forschungsamt* report I have discovered that Swedish newspapers have used every means at their disposal to resist publishing the reports from their Berlin correspondents [about the Katyn massacres of Polish officers]. One can see again from this how little Sweden really is neutral. Here too the Jews are at work, and the Swedish Philistines do what the Jews recommend or order them to do. One wishes that they would try a sojourn in a Bolshevik mass grave next time they have the chance; there is no other way of bringing the Philistines in neutral countries to their senses.

22 April 1943

I have learned from telephone conversations and diplomatic reports intercepted by the *Forschungsamt* that Rome would like to see more emphasis placed on the discussions on Europe than we have employed from our side so far. A telephone conversation between Laval and Brinon expresses the same wish. Apart from this, I see from the latter telephone conversation that the wife of our Ambassador Abetz has made very rash remarks to French diplomats. She is of course a French-woman—yet another example of the need for diplomats not to marry except among their own compatriots.

23 April 1943

From the reports of the *Forschungsamt* I see that the Rumanians are not nearly as enthusiastic about the meetings they have had [with Hitler and von Ribbentrop] on the Obersalzberg as we have supposed. They missed a clear sense of purpose in German foreign policy and the German war effort.

17 May 1943

The Americans are now in the process of making extremely severe attacks on Moscow. The Soviets have shown themselves rather too inflexible towards Roosevelt's wishes. I can see from the *Forschungsamt's* monitoring reports that Roosevelt is using extremely powerful language to the Kremlin. [Ambassador] Davies' special mission is said to be to blackmail Stalin into meeting Roosevelt and Churchill, failing which radical new decisions will be taken on the Anglo-American war effort.

23 May 1943

From the *Forschungsamt* I have received material on the object of Churchill's visit to Washington. From this too it can be seen that Churchill's intention is to mediate between Stalin and Roosevelt. Roosevelt has evidently lost some of the support of his public because of his strong association with Bolshevism. Thus he must pick up some support so that politically speaking he can walk without assistance again. Apart from this the *Forschungsamt* reports reproduce a whole series of rumours of which the one contradicts the other.

26 May 1943

From the *Forschungsamt's* monitoring reports I have gained a clear insight into the mentality of Roosevelt's Ambassador Davies, who is at present posted to Kuibyshev. From this he is seen to be a convinced ally of the Soviet Union, who is the more dangerous as he springs from arch-capitalistic circles, has married into a million dollars and seeks nothing more than to make a good career for himself. He is a dangerously ignorant man who is inflicting serious damage on any clearly defined and realistic foreign policy. We must see in him a kind of drawing-room Bolshevist: and on these drawing-room Bolshevists we must think with the language of the Bible—may we forgive them, for they know not what they are doing. The abundance of his naïvety is shown by the belief he has expressed in conversation with diplomats at Kuibyshev, that M. Stalin is fighting this war with no desire for territorial gain. In the Kremlin they must be greeting this American diplomatic dilet-tante with Homeric laughter. If Davies describes himself as an un-restricted admirer of Marshal Stalin, it shows that this plutocratic diplomat has not the smallest inkling of what today's world is about.

Other intercepted diplomatic reports from Ankara prove that Turkey intends to hang grimly on to her neutral position until the war is over if possible. The main reason given is that Turkish statesmen realise the necessity of maintaining their armed forces intact at the end of the war, in order to be able to ward off possible encroachments by the Soviet Union.

Other monitored telephone conversations show the Italian Ambas-sador in Berlin, Alfieri, to be of such vanity that I am forced to smile.

2 November 1943

Through Ankara we have received reports that Maisky and Litvinov can by and large be regarded as having been deposed. They have been overthrown by Vishinsky, who is now Stalin's most trusted foreign affairs adviser after Molotov. That Stalin has sacked the Jews, of all people, is explained by the fact that in the plutocratic countries they had been mingling too freely with capitalistic circles. They were too accommodating towards Churchill and Roosevelt, and that did not tally with Stalin's ideas.

13 November 1943

I have now received confidential material bearing upon the Moscow conference. From this it can be seen that Stalin has categorically de-manded the opening of the Second Front. The British and Americans are not in a position to meet this demand at present. They therefore have to be satisfied with a promise from Stalin that he will not make a separate peace with the Reich. For this, the British have been obliged to refrain from launching any operations in the Balkans. No agreement has been achieved on Poland or even on the Baltic States and Finland, since the Soviets have not permitted any discussion whatsoever on these topics. All told, Britain and America have lost heavily at the Moscow conference. Here and there in the diplomatic reports there is a suggestion that the British plutocrats are toying with the idea of changing their overall policies towards the Soviet Union. I cannot believe that this is true, but it still seems interesting to me that such things can even be thought of now.

At Menememcioglu's request, Eden has had talks with him in Cairo. While there, he advised him of the Soviet demand for military bases in Turkey. Menememcioglu has turned down this demand, and pointed out that the various constitutional bodies would have to be asked first of all, particularly the Turkish People's Party. Eden represented the Soviet case only half-heartedly, and did not make it at all difficult for Turkey to reject them. When Menememcioglu objected that if military bases were to be permitted in Turkey this would result in armed intervention by the Reich, Eden answered that the Reich was today in no position to do that—for which the Azores operation provided adequate example. The British seem to have got rather cold feet over the Soviet demands on Turkey. In any event there is no suggestion that Turkey should be put under some kind of blackmail.

Reich Air Ministry   Sample
Forschungsamt

Secret

OATH OF SECRECY AND DISCRETION

I the undersigned   (Christian and Surname) witness by my own hand that I will maintain absolute secrecy and discretion with respect to what I have seen, heard or learned of the aims, functions, activity, affairs and premises of the *Forschungsamt*. This undertaking is given without any limitation with respect to time.

I am aware that I may discuss this only with those persons (whether superiors or subordinates) and departments who are also sworn to secrecy about the *Forschungsamt*, and who have been appointed to assist me, and only when it is absolutely necessary in the line of duty.

Release from this Oath of Secrecy, even to testify in Court and for similar purposes, can only be granted by the *Forschungsamt*. I also regard myself as bound to bring directly to the *Forschungsamt's* attention any breaches of its secrecy by others that may come to my ears.

I am aware that breaches of this undertaking will result either in disciplinary measures or in prosecution for accidental, deliberate or attempted betrayal of State Secrets under paras. 88 to 93 of the Reich Penal Code and the confiscation of my property, custody, gaol, penal servitude or the death penalty.

Countersigned: Signed:

(Christian and Surname)   (Christian and Surname).

IVa

Reich Air Ministry
Forschungsamt
—I—795 42 Top Secret

Copy No. 01178

Top Secret

INSTRUCTIONS ON THE SECRECY OF INTERCEPT MATERIALS FROM THE FORSCHUNGSAMT (FA) AT DEPARTMENTAL LEVEL*

A. *General*

1. The work of the FA is of value and purpose only if its secrecy is maintained by all possible means. Insufficient security will lead to the enemy taking precautions and the loss of our sources will result.

2. The methods and functions of the FA and the intercepted material resulting are State Secrets in the sense of para. 88 of the Reich Penal Code (RPC). The intercept materials (the 'Brown Pages' and Reports, and the individual reports and summaries as well) are 'Top Secret' for security regulation purposes insofar as they are not classified only as 'Secret'. The disclosure of the secrets of intercept materials, their origin and contents endangers the security of the State; violations of the oath of secrecy will be punished as high treason (paras. 88 to 93 of the RCP).

3. It is desired that the head of each department receiving the FA's intercept documents should nominate a reliable representative or liaison officer (LO) for FA matters within his own department, and that this name should be forwarded to the FA. In special cases—for example where a very large volume of intercept materials is supplied to several offices within the one department, the FA will provide its own liaison officer (LO). The LO's are responsible for processing and surrendering intercept materials.

* [This document from German Army High Command files, shows the extent to which the *Forschungsamt* went to keep its methods and existence secret from the German public and the enemy. The reports it circulated were termed *Forschungsergebnisse*, which has been translated here not literally as 'research data' but with its intended meaning of 'intercepted materials' or 'intercepted documents'.]

4. *a*) Everybody, including the department head and his deputy, who is aware of the FA, its methods and its functions, or who is engaged in the receipt or handling of the intercept materials, is to be bound by an oath of secrecy and discretion. The general obligation of secrecy is not a substitute for the special secrecy and discretion undertaking required in connection with all the FA's affairs; the latter undertaking is supplementary in every case, and no person is allowed to refuse to give such an undertaking.

(*b*) The departmental head, his deputy and every person required to see or handle intercept material, must be authorised by name for that purpose by the FA. The user permit includes authorisation to receive (see para. 4*a*).

(*c*) The recipient permit issued by name by the FA authorises *only* the acceptance of and signing for sealed pouches, folders or envelopes containing intercept materials; it does *not* authorise the opening, reading or use of their contents.

5. Departments are requested to make application applications under para. 4. The need for signed undertakings on secrecy (see para. 4*a*) must be brought to the notice of the FA by the department, or vice versa. Applications for recipient or user permits are to be made in writing to the *Forschungsamt* on the forms provided and signed by the department head or his deputy (see para. 18).

6. The execution of the Oath of Secrecy is to be on the basis of the printed form of Oath (see Sample)★ and, if the same person is to be given a user permit, on the basis of the Instructions on the Secrecy of Intercept Materials, and of the Extract from the Regulations for Control of Intercept Materials;† the ceremony is to be performed by the LO of the FA or by an FA representative. Every person authorised as a user is to be handed against a signed receipt one copy each of the Instructions and of the Extract, and every person authorised as a receeipient a copy of the Extract.

In fulfilment of the applications for recipient or user permits, the FA will arrange the supply of intercept materials concerned, subject to the Reichsmarschall's (i.e. Hermann Goring's) consent.

7. In accordance with the 'Basic Command of the Fuhrer' (on security of State secrets) the number of those bound to secrecy, or authorised as users or recipients, is to be limited to an absolute minimum. Basically only senior civil servants or officers are to be authorised as users. Exceptions must remain exceptions and must have special justification.

★ Printed on page 184.   † See Appendix IVb, page 190.

Every change of status of the signatories, users and recipients (e.g. change of office or rank) must be notified to the FA at once (see para. 18).

8. Requests for monitoring are always to be directed in writing to the FA, accompanied by the precise reasons and the signature of the department head or his deputy (see paras. 16 and 18). The monitoring and supply of the results thereof will be performed by the FA subject to the instructions and consent of the Reichsmarschall. In forwarding such requests, unambiguous wording and the precise description of the reason and purpose are necessary, in order that the applicant's intentions can be satisfied in the best and most logical manner possible. It is also strongly urged that applications should be cancelled immediately the applicant regards them as completed.

B. *Handling of Intercept Materials, Correspondence, and Co-operation between the FA and other departments.*

9. Transmission of intercept materials between the FA and departments is performed by the FA's own special couriers in pouches fastened with a special safety lock or by its internal pneumatic post system, and in urgent instances by cipher teleprinters, insofar as delivery cannot be effected by an FA liaison office. Exceptions from this exclusive transmission by FA-couriers, which is provided in the interests of security and secrecy, may be made only in specially arranged instances after the FA's express agreement has been secured.

It is absolutely forbidden to transmit or discuss the FA's intercept materials on the public telephone. The receipt of pouches, folders or envelopes is to be signed for by the recipient in the courier's receipt book. The authorised user is to confirm receipt of intercept documents on the special red receipt-certificate inside, or in the receipt book kept in the liaison office.

10. The forwarding either in original or copy of intercept documents classified as 'Top Secret' (e.g. the 'Brown Pages') outside the circle of persons authorised to use them is prohibited without exception. To other persons—i.e. those not authorised to use intercept materials— the content of these documents (for example the 'Brown Pages') may be made known only in extract and in paraphrase, in other words not quoted verbatim, and only after every indication of their origin and method of procurement has been suppressed and provided that these persons are the competent officials concerned. In this instance the

material forwarded still come under the secrecy regulations. The departmental head is responsible for material made available elsewhere.

11. Safekeeping of intercept materials and all documents relating to them is to be such that under no circumstances can unauthorised persons gain access to them (steel cabinet or safe). In no case may intercept documents and materials lie open in the room or on the desk, or be kept in wooden containers (cupboards or drawers). (See Secrecy Regulations.) It is strictly forbidden to take intercept materials home or on public transport.

12. Intercept materials classified as 'Top Secret' and no longer required are to be returned to the FA at regular intervals, and will be destroyed here. Those intercept materials classified as 'Secret' are to be destroyed by the recipients themselves on their own responsibility, if they are not returned to the FA.

13. All persons receiving or forwarding intercept materials must be in a position to prove the receipt, possession or forwarding of same. The LO of the department or FA is to maintain a special written register of all intercept materials, their distribution, forwarding, safekeeping and return or destruction, and must be able to produce it for scrutiny at all times.

14. In cases of suspected or confirmed loss of intercept materials the FA is to be advised at once (see para. 18). The FA's counter-espionage officer will immediately contact the department concerned to co-ordinate their investigation. In addition, the procedures laid down in paras. 27 and 28 of Secrecy Regulations are to be observed.

15. The above regulations also apply to correspondence about intercept materials and the related problems. Such correspondence may under no circumstances follow the normal channels but must take place solely between the department head, liaison officer or an authorised user at one end, and the FA at the other end. For the FA's address in this case see para. 18. For this reason a particularly trustworthy secretary, provided solely for this purpose, must be allocated for correspondence. This secretary is also to be sworn to secrecy by the special procedure. An internal letter-register is to be kept on this correspondence, from which the letter's whereabouts must be ascertainable at any time.

16. Use of the public telephone for reports on the content of intercept documents and related matters is strictly forbidden. Such conversations may be made only with particular caution and on the special telephone lines of the FA. Cipher-teleprinters and internal (FA) pneumatic post are also permissible.

17. Departments will give real support to the FA in its work if they not only conform closely with the regulations but also actively co-operate, in their own interests. This includes inter alia: provision of pertinent supplementary information, corrections, confirmation and conclusions from the documents they receive; and also making available Intelligence they procure themselves—foreign codes, ciphers, keys and other secret communications methods that come into their hands. Pointers to further Intelligence sources and special events as well as reports of successful operations and their own plans and intentions will be very valuable for the FA's work.

It must also be borne in mind that the initiations of unilateral actions as a result of FA reports can easily cause important FA sources to dry up. On the other hand, the presence of, or collaboration of an FA officer at interrogations, interviews, confiscation of property, etc., can lead to the securing of new and valuable source material.

C. *Addresses and Telephone Numbers.*

18. At present the following addresses and telephone numbers are in force for the *Forschungsamt:*

Forschungsamt of the Reich Air Ministry, Berlin-Charlottenburg 2, Schillerstrasse 116–124. Telephone: 31 00 15 (only for simple conversations!).

Director: Ministerial-Director the Prince of Hesse.

Deputy: Ministerial-Dirigent Schapper.

For matters connected with Intercept materials and requests:
  Ministerialrat Seifert
  Deputy: Oberregierungsrat Dr Kurzbach.

For matters connected with Security, Secrecy, Counter-Espionage and the Loss of Intercept Documents:
  Oberregierungsrat Rosenhahn
  Deputy: Regierungsrat Proksch

On Sundays, outside office hours and at night:
  Senior duty officer of the F.A.

Conversations of secret content only on the special telephone lines provided for this purpose! (See para. 16).

19. Departments provided by the FA with intercept documents and with these regulations are to notify to the FA: departmental address and telephone number and those of its designated representative and of his deputy, and of their availability in emergencies on Sundays, after office hours and at night. The FA is to be kept informed of all alterations.

IVb

Reich Air Ministry
Forschungsamt
-I-797J42 Top Secret

Copy No. 00944

Top Secret

EXTRACT FROM REGULATIONS ON THE CONTROL OF INTERCEPTED MATERIALS OF THE FA

1. Competence and Function: The control of all intercept materials distributed by the Forschungsamt is the responsibility of the FA.

2. Recipients: A list of offices and persons authorised as recipients is kept by the FA. Only authorised recipients may sign for receipt of intercept materials. The liaison officer is to transmit intercept materials only to authorised recipients.

3. Certificate of Receipt: Every intercept document received is to be signed for without exception.

4. Restitution and Withdrawal:

(*a*) All intercept materials bearing the classification 'Top Secret' are to be returned without fail to the liaison office. If necessary the *Forschungsamt's* liaison office is to remind recipients of their obligation to return them, and it is to be in a position to recover earlier reports by means of following the serial numbers of the items. Those intercept materials classified as 'Secret' are to be destroyed by the recipients themselves if they are not returned to the *Forschungsamt's* liaison office.

(*b*) The return of the previous month's materials at the beginning of the following month is desired.

Notes and Sources

For the sake of general readability, some of the annotations in the original document have been resited in the body of the text, but those principally disclosing the source of the information—the Brown Pages' serial numbers, and usually a description of their origin—have been printed below. The present Editor's comments are included in square brackets.

Part I

1 [The Anglo-German Declaration was the famous 'piece of paper' waved by Chamberlain at Heston airport after his return by air from Munich.]

2 [*Hansard's Parliamentary Debates*, Fifth Series (hereafter cited as *H.C. Deb*). vol. 339, cols. 40–56. Some minor passages have been omitted in the German text, and they have not been included here.]

3 [These sources include the following:] N. 98,186: [telephone conversation between] Henderson and [Italian Ambassador] Attolico about François-Poncet's visit to the Führer on 4 October [1938]; Henderson informed Attolico that the Führer had protested to François-Poncet that the British and French delegates were trying to sabotage the Munich Agreement.
N. 98,908: report from Agence d'Espagne, Paris, dated 1 October.
N. 98,911: [telephone conversation between] Kirkpatrick and Foreign Office, 5 October.
N. 99,132: ditto, François-Poncet with Henry, Quai d'Orsay, 5 October.

N. 99,630: ditto, François-Poncet with Henderson, 11 October.
N. 99,380: ditto, François-Poncet with Henderson, 7 October.
N. 99,447: ditto, Counsellor of Legation Schubert with Mastny [Czech Minister in Berlin] on subject of Chamberlain's statement in the House of Commons on 7 October. [This must be an error for 3 October: the Commons were not in session on the 7th, having adjourned on the previous day until 1 November 1938, as is evident from *H.C. Deb.*, vol. 339, col. 562.] [For Sir Nevile Henderson's account of the meetings of the International Commission, see his *Failure of a Mission*, (Hodder and Stoughton, London, 1941) pp. 168–70. Mastny was the Czech delegate to this Commission.]

4 N. 99,116.

5 N. 99,186: Foreign Office instruction to the British Embassy in Berlin, dated 5 October. [No reference to this telegram appears in the published series of official British documents (see Note 11) or in those published by the inter-allied project from German sources (see Note 21).]

6 N. 98,871 [telephone conversation

between Henderson and Attolico, 2 October 1938.]

7 N. 98,859.

8 N. 98,937, N. 99, 313.

9 N. 99,186 [see Note 5. Hitler spoke at the Sportpalast on 5 October. In the course of this speech he attacked Duff Cooper and Eden by name: cf. Max Domarus, *Hitler—Reden und Proklamationen 1932–45* (Neustadt, 1962) vol. I, pp. 950–2.]

10 N. 105,906 [report of Japanese Ambassador in London to Tokyo, dated 16 December 1938].

11 N. 102,515 [telegram from Lord Halifax to British Embassy in Berlin, 11 November 1938 (see *Documents on British Foreign Policy*, Third Series, vol III, no. 302. Cited hereafter as *D.B.F.P.*) The German diplomatist vom Rath was murdered by a German Jewish refugee, Herschel von Grynzpan.]

12 [The relevant sentence in Halifax's telegram of 11 November 1938 reads: 'The publication of these scurrilous attacks is indefensible and is moreover in harmony neither with the spirit of my conversation with Dr Goebbels in Berlin last November nor with the intention of the Declaration which the Prime Minister and Chancellor signed in Munich "to continue our efforts to remove every possible source of difference".']

13 [See *H.C. Deb.*, vol. 341, cols. 503–6.]

14 [In his speech, Chamberlain said: 'It takes two to make an Agreement, just as it takes two to make a war, and I am still waiting for a sign from those who speak for the German people that they share this desire, and that they are prepared to make their contribution to the peace, which would help them as much as it would help us.'—*H.C. Deb.*, vol. 342, cols. 2517–26.]

15 It is worth recording in this context a remark by the Polish Ambassador in Paris, Lukasiewicz, to the effect that the British and French nations had been exceptionally loath to make war [at Munich], and for this reason they had thrown their conservative policies to the wind and agreed in the long run to a compromise. (Report of Japanese Ambassador in Paris, Sugimura [to Tokyo], N. 99,640.)

16 N. 105,906 [report of Japanese Ambassador in London, Shigemitsu, to Tokyo, dated 16 December 1938].

17 [On 26 January 1939 M. Bonnet stated in a speech to the French Chamber of Deputies that in the event of a war in which both Britain and France were involved, the forces of Great Britain would be at the disposal of France just as the forces of France would be at the disposal of Great Britain. *H.C. Deb.*, vol. 343, col. 623.]

18 [Mr Robert Hudson, Parliamentary Secretary to the Department of Overseas Trade, visited Warsaw and Moscow late in March 1939 for conversations on 'trade matters'.]

19 [No reference to these 'negotiations' appears in the published series of official British documents.]

20 [see *H.C. Deb.*, vol. 345, cols. 221–4.]

21 No. 112,097 [see *D.B.F.P.*, vol. IV, nos. 247 and 264. See also

Documents on German Foreign Policy, Series D, vol. IV, no. 234 (cited hereafter as *D.G.F.P.*).]

22 [Chamberlain stated in his speech: 'His Majesty's Government feel bound to say that this [attempt by the German Government to dominate Europe by successive steps] would rouse the successful resistance of this and other countries who prize their freedom, as similar attempts have done in the past.' See *H.C. Deb.*, vol. 345, col. 1462.]

23 [For the text of Chamberlain's speech at Birmingham see Command Paper (Cmd.) no. 6106 (1939) No. 9.]

24 N. 112,548 [report of Momtchiloff to Sofia.]

25 [See *Hansard's Parliamentary Debates*, Fifth Series, *House of Lords*, vol. 112, cols. 308–19.]

26 *V.N. Nr.* 1859/3. 39. [*Vertrauliche Nachrichten* (Confidential information) were the deciphered documents circulated by the cryptanalysis section of the German High Command, *OKW/Chi*. Three samples of these, including a cable from the U.S. Secretary of State Stettinius to the American Consulate in Tunis, dated 29 December 1944, can be found in *OKW* file 1707, microfilmed on National Archives film T-77, roll 1456, frames 201–3. For the document described by *V.N. Nr.*1859/3. 39, see *D.B.F.P.*, vol IV, no. 308 and 401; and *D.G.F.P.*, vol. VI, no. 26.]

27 [Sir Nevile Henderson actually left Berlin on 18 March; see *D.B.F.P.* vol IV, no. 308 footnote 2.]

28 [See *D.G.F.P.*, vol VI, no. 25, footnote 2.]

Part II

1 N. 112,581.

2 N. 112,264.

3 N. 112,548: information from Yugoslav Foreign Minister[Cincar-Markovic] to Yugoslav Minister in Berlin.

4 [See *H.C. Deb.*, vol. 345, cols. 1883–5.]

5 N. 115,433.

6 N. 114,473.

7 N. 115,068. In this connection a broadcast transmitted by Daventry on 24 June is worthy of comment. It was stated in this that it had been reported from Bucharest that Gafencu was working on a mutual assistance plan designed to embrace Rumania, Yugoslavia, Turkey and Greece.

8 N. 114,876: information from Yugoslav Foreign Minister for the Yugoslav Minister in Berlin, about conversation between Mavroudis and the Yugoslav Minister in Athens.

9 N. 114,524 [report by Bulgarian Counsellor Dragutinovic from Geneva, 4 April 1939].

10 In a radio broadcast, the Professor of International Relations at Oxford, Sir Alfred Zimmern, said that the important strategic factor in the new Anglo-Turkish Treaty was that Turkey controlled the access to the Black Sea. Turkey had finally coupled her destiny with that of Britain, and had relinquished the policies she had pursued since 1914 (RW. 213).

11 N. 106,111 [report by Yugoslav Minister in Ankara, Adzemovic, 23 December 1938, on a conversation with de Peppo].

12 N. 117,395 [report by Yugoslav Counsellor of Legation Milanovic in London, 9 April 1939, on a conversation with [Turkish] Ambassador Rüstü Aras].

13 N. 116,206 [brief from Turkish Foreign Minister to Turkish Embassy in Moscow, dated 27 April 1939. See *D.B.F.P.*, vol V. nos. 219, 239, 260, 271, 276, 286, 287, 291 and 308. In a telegram to the British Ambassador on 22 April 1939 (No. 260), Lord Halifax said: 'It must be made quite clear, however, that what is said in any staff conversations which may take place between His Majesty's Government and the Turkish Government is for Turkish ears only.']

14 N. 115,599. [See *D.B.F.P.*, vol. V, nos. 155, 190, 191, 199 and 200. The actual text of the Turkish reply quoted here, as transmitted in French to the British Foreign Office by M. Rüstü Aras, the Turkish Ambassador in London, is printed in ibid., No. 199. The Germans were unable to break down some passages of the Turkish cable's code, and left appropriate gaps, indicated in our text by dots. For a facsimile of the German text see page 14.]

15 When a Turkish military mission visited London in June 1939 for talks on the supply of war materials, the head of this mission, General Orbay, reported that in view of possible difficulties in transporting to Turkey the material to be supplied by Britain, there was a plan to obtain all the material asked of Britain from Russian sources instead. Orbay added a comment that Britain would only be able to satisfy a part of the Turkish requirements, as she was faced with the needs and demands of her own Army and the armies of her allies and of the Eastern Front (N. 121, 213).

16 The Declaration was read out by Mr Chamberlain in the House of Commons in London (Cf. *Monatshefte für auswärtige Politik*, No. 6, p. 599). [See *H.C. Deb.*, vol. 347, cols. 952–6, which contains the text of the Anglo-Turkish Declaration of 12 May 1939.]

17 The Treaty was not finally signed until 19 October 1939, after the outbreak of war.

18 N. 117,893.

19 N. 122,104.

20 N. 119,439 [In view of Turkish complaints made at the end of June 1939 that no war material had as yet reached Turkey from Britain, this report would seem to be quite inaccurate. See *D.B.F.P.*, vol V, Nos. 239, 512; vol. VI, nos. 98, 168.]

21 Article Six of the Declaration of 12 May 1939 states: 'The two Governments recognize that it is also necessary to ensure the establishment of security in the Balkans and they are consulting together with the object of achieving this purpose as speedily as possible.' [For Anglo-Turkish correspondence on this Article, see *D.B.F.P.*, vol V, nos. 391–6, 423 and 444.]

22 N. 121,727 [despatch from Yugoslav Legation in Ankara, dated 1 July 1939].

23 N. 112,905: information from Yugoslav Foreign Minister Cincar-Markovic for the Yugoslav chargé d'affaires in Berlin, 21 March 1939. [See *D.B.F.P.*, vol. IV, nos. 389, 390 and 395. For extracts from M. Tilea's account of this interview and for the instructions on which he acted see V. Mosiuc, *Tratatul economic românogerman dur 23 Marte 1939 si semnificatie sa*, printed in *Analele*, vol. XII, no. 4, 1967, pp. 130–46 (particularly p. 135). See also M. Tilea's letter in the *Daily Telegraph*, 21 February 1963.]

24 N. 114,491: information from Yugoslav Foreign Minister, Cincar-Markovic, for the Yugoslav Legation in Berlin, 6 April 1939. [The initiative in issuing the declaration to Rumania actually came from the Rumanian side. See *D.B.F.P.*, vol. IV, nos. 558, 587, 603; and ibid., vol. V, nos. 9, 15, 30, 40, 41, 44, 54, and 65.]

25 [No serial-number is given for Chigi's despatch.]

26 *DNB* Anglo 13 April, page 18. [The reference is to a report of the *Deutsche Nachrichten Büro*, the official German news agency. We have based our translation on the original text printed in *H.C. Deb.*, vol. 346, col 13, except that the German text refers to 'the British' government, where *Hansard* refers to 'His Majesty's' government, and the German text's minor omissions have also been followed here.]

27 N. 115,826 [report by Yugoslav Minister in Paris, Puric, to the Foreign Ministry in Belgrade, 21 April]. A further item in Puric's report is worth recording here—a statement attributed to the Polish Ambassador in Paris, Lukasiewicz, that neither Rumania nor Poland desired any Treaty against Germany, as they did not wish to provoke her; and that each of these two countries was

hoping that Germany would set about the other.

28 [For the British version of M. Gafencu's conversations in London, see *D.B.F.P.*, vol. V, nos. 278, 279, 285, 295. M. Gafencu's memories of these conversations are to be found in G. Gafencu, *The Last Days of Europe*, (London, 1948) pp. 113–24.]

29 According to a despatch filed by the Japanese Ambassador in London, Shigemitsu, Britain agreed to a loan of £5 millions; Shigemitsu pointed out that as Rumania had originally asked for £30 millions, the small size of this loan had been received with disappointment in Rumania (N. 119,222).

30 N. 115,959.

31 N. 116,202.

32 [Hitler's alleged words are not reproduced either in the German record of his conversation of 19 April 1939 with Gafencu, or in the British record of Gafencu's account of the meeting. See *D.G.F.P.*, vol. VI, no. 234, and *D.B.F.P.*, vol. V, no. 278; see also Gafencu, pp. 65–79. On the other hand, in a conference with Cincar-Markovic on 25 April 1939, von Ribbentrop stated that Hitler had sought only friendship with Great Britain, and Rumania had been duly informed of the 'worthless' character of the recent British guarantee to that country. See U.S. State Department interrogation of Dr Paul Schmidt, 31 October 1945.]

33 A despatch from the Bulgarian Minister in Paris, Balabanoff, to the Foreign Minister in Sofia, dated 29 April 1939, about Gafencu's visits to London and Paris agrees with the

Yugoslav information described in the text.

34 N. 119,222.

35 [No serial-number is given for Sumenkovic's despatch.]

36 For its text see page 24 above.

37 N. 114,750 [report by Yugoslav Minister in Warsaw, Vukcevic, dated 11 April 1939].

38 N. 114,876.

39 N. 114,876: information from Yugoslav Foreign Minister, Cincar-Marcovic, to Yugoslav Minister in Berlin, 11 April 1939. [The reports referred to do not correspond with the evidence contained in the published British official documents. According to the British record, the decision to give a guarantee to Greece only took on concrete form on 9 April after a report—originating from the Greek military attaché in Rome—of an imminent Italian attack on the Greek island of Corfu, which Italy had attacked before, in 1923. This report was communicated at midnight on 8–9 April by the Greek premier to the British Minister in Athens. Turkish doubts as to the firmness of British intentions, reported on 10 April by the British Ambassador in Ankara, strengthened this decision, which was communicated to the Greek government for the first time on 12 April. The guarantee was announced in the House of Commons on 13 April 1939, together with that given to Rumania.]

40 N. 114,715 [report of Yugoslav Minister in London to Belgrade, 12 April 1939].

41 N. 119,222 [report of Japanese Ambassador in London, Shigemitsu, to Tokyo, dated 30 May 1939].

42 N. 115,068 [report of Bulgarian Minister in London, Momtchiloff, 15 April 1939. Initial British interest in the settlement of Bulgaria's dispute with Turkey and Rumania was, in fact, expressed on 12 April during the Anglo-Turkish discussions leading to the Anglo-Turkish Declaration of 12 May 1939. From the official British documents it would appear that the initiative in approaching Bulgaria was left to the Turkish government. See *D.B.F.P.*, vol. V, nos. 62, 63, 138, 162.]

43 N. 115,433. [There is no record of a conversation of Momtchiloff in the Foreign Office on 17 April in the published series of official British documents.]

44 N. 115,433: despatch from Yugoslav chargé d'affaires in London, Milanovic, to the Foreign Ministry in Belgrade, 18 April 1939. In this despatch Milanovic reported that he had gained the impression from his conversation with Momtchiloff that Bulgaria wanted to exploit the British diplomatic activity to secure a frontier change in Dobruja, and that she wanted moreover to achieve a solution later to the question of access to the Aegean Sea.

45 N. 114,707: information from Yugoslav Foreign Minister Cincar-Markovic for the Yugoslav Legation in Berlin, 11 April 1939, about a despatch from the Yugoslav Legation in Sofia. [No record of such a conversation between Mr George Rendel, the British Minister in Sofia, and M. Kiosseivanoff, the Bulgarian Prime Minister, appears in the published official British documents. Assuming the Yugoslav report to be accurate, the timing would suggest that Mr Rendel was acting on his own initiative as the initial British enquiry in this sense was only made to the Turkish authorities on 12 April. Mr Rendel was, naturally, kept *au courant* with the progress of the British guarantee negotiations with Greece.]

46 N. 115,782: information from Yugoslav Foreign Minister Cincar-Markovic for Yugoslav Legation in Berlin on 22 April, about a despatch from their Legation in Sofia. [No record of such a conversation between Mr Rendel and M. Kiosseivanoff appears in the official British documents. Indeed, on 14 April M. Tilea, the Rumanian Minister in London, was assured by Sir Alexander Cadogan, Permanent Under-Secretary in the British Foreign Office, that the initiative in Rumanian-Bulgarian matters would be left to the Rumanian authorities whom Sir Alexander urged to make concessions to Bulgaria. Similar arguments were urged on M. Gafencu during his visit to London. See *D.B.F.P.*, vol. V, nos. 173, 278, 279 and 285.]

47 For example M. Sokoline, the Soviet Secretary-General at the League of Nations, is said to have commented that Britain intervened several times in Bucharest on Bulgaria's behalf (Report by the Yugoslav delegate at the League of Nations, Soubotic, from Geneva, 25 May 1939: N. 118,938).

48 N. 116,490: report of Bulgarian Minister in Paris, Balabanoff, 29 April 1939. [See also Note 46.]

49 N. 115,767: information from Yugoslav Foreign Minister Cincar-Markovic for the Yugoslav Legation in Berlin, about a report from the Yugoslav Legation in Athens, dated 20 April 1939. [No record of any such Anglo-Greek conversations appears in the published series of official British documents before 22 April 1939. See *D.B.F.P.*, vol. V, no. 299.]

50 N. 118,105. [See Note 51].

51 N. 123,506: despatch by Yugoslav Legation in London to the Foreign Ministry in Belgrade, 16 May 1939, about a conversation with the Bulgarian Minister in London (N. 118,105). [The *Forschungsamt* report appears to have confused the serial-numbers of these two sources.]

52 N. 122,419.

53 N. 123,506. [See Note 51.] [For Kiosseivanoff's visit to Berlin on 5–6 July, see *D.G.F.P.*, vol. VI nos. 617 and 618. See also *D.B.F.P.*, vol. VI, nos. 310 and 311; and for the British record of a conversation between Lord Halifax and M. Mashanoff on 20 July 1939, see *D.B. F.P.*, vol VI. no. 393 footnote 3. For other material on M. Mashanoff's visit to London see (*I*) *Documenti Diplomatici Italiani*, Ottava Serie, vol. XII (Cited hereafter as *D.D.I.*)].

54 N. 123,702: report from Bulgarian Minister in London, Momtchiloff, to the Foreign Ministry in Sofia, 25 August 1939. [The British Government do not in fact appear to have taken up any initiative on this issue before the outbreak of war.]

55 In an interview granted to the London correspondent of the Czech Press Agency C.T.K., Mme Dr

Worlicek, on 14 October 1937, Stoyadinovic stated that the March 1937 agreement with Italy had bestowed on Yugoslavia the benefits of the Rome Protocol's preferences without Yugoslavia's having had to join the three Powers of the Rome Protocol, or even having had to express the intention of doing so. The British 'gentlemen's agreement' of 12 January 1937 had been the prerequisite and simultaneously the basis for the Yugoslav Italian Treaty. Yugoslavia's policies in the Mediterranean were in harmony with Britain's policies there.

56 [A conference was held at Nyons from 10 to 14 September 1937 on measures to counter attacks by 'unknown'—in fact Italian—submarines on shipping in the Mediterranean during the Spanish Civil War.]

57 N. 71,962.

58 N. 122,823 [report of Yugoslav Minister in Sofia, 13 July 1939].

59 N. 123,001 [report of Bulgarian Minister in London, Momtchiloff, 2 August 1939]. In this context a despatch by the Bulgarian Minister in Berlin, Draganoff, to the Foreign Ministry in Sofia, dated 21 July 1939, is of some interest: this states that the London visit [of Prince Paul] had made an unfavourable impression in Berlin—it had convinced the Foreign Ministry that Yugoslavia was not a reliable partner, and that she wanted to play a double role [*an zwei Tischen spielen*] to the very end (N. 122, 911). [For Prince Paul's visit to Berlin and German reactions to his subsequent visits to London, see *D.G.F.P.*, vol. VI, nos.

474, 680, 688 and 691. For the British record of a conversation between Lord Halifax and Prince Paul, see *D.B.F.P.*, vol. VI, no. 393.]

60 N. 123,782 [report of Japanese Consul-General in Vienna, Yamji, to Foreign Ministry in Tokyo, 3 August 1939].

61 N. 123,373 [report of Bulgarian Minister in London to Foreign Ministry in Sofia, 2 August 1939].

62 N. 124,673 [information of Yugoslav Foreign Minister for Yugoslav Legation in Berlin, 13 August 1939].

63 [No record of such a conversation appears in the published German documents. The reports printed in the text do not accord with anything in the printed British documents.]

64 Which confirms the report (summarised on page 57 above) about the point of time at which the British consultations on encirclement began. [See *D.B.F.P.*, vol. IV, nos. 389 and 403.]

65 [As noted in our Introduction, the German Embassy in London appears to have disposed of much more accurate Intelligence of the course of Anglo-Soviet negotiations than the *Forschungsamt* could extract from foreign diplomatic cables.]

66 N. 115,968 [despatch from Turkish Ambassador in Moscow, Apaydin, to Foreign Ministry in Ankara, 21 April 1939].

67 N. 116,207: report from Milanovic to Belgrade, 26 April 1939. [The published British records of the Anglo-Soviet negotiations do not contain any reference to the Far East.]

68 N. 115,968: report from Apaydin,

dated 21 April 1939; and N. 117, 393: report from Yugoslav chargé d'affaires in London, 9 May 1939. [The reference would appear to be to the Soviet proposals of 18 April 1939. See *D.B.F.P.*, vol. VI, no. 201.]

69 N. 116,207 [report of Yugoslav chargé d'affaires in London, Milanovic, 26 April 1939].

70 N. 118,900 [report of Turkish Ambassador in Moscow, Apaydin, 24 May 1939].

71 N. 118,213: information from Turkish Foreign Minister Saracoglu for Turkish Ambassador in London, Rüstü Aras, 17 May 1939. [The reference would appear to be to the Soviet proposals of 14 May 1939. See *D.B.F.P.*, vol. V, no. 520.]

72 N. 117,395: report of Yugoslav chargé d'affaires in London, Milanovic, 9 May 1939. [This would appear to be another garbled version of the British proposals 6 May 1939. See *D.B.F.P.*, vol. V, nos. 389 and 397]

73 N. 121,916: report from Turkish Ambassador in Rome, Baydur, 6 July 1939, on information obtained from the British Ambassador, [Sir Percy] Loraine. [A reference to the British proposals of 25 May 1939. See *D.B.F.P.*, vol. V, nos, 624 and 625.]

74 N. 119,552: report of Latvian Minister in London, Zarine, 6 June 1939. [See also *D.B.F.P.*, vol. V, nos, 610, 646, 674, 710 and 711.]

75 N. 122,918: [telephone?] conversation between U.S. Ambassador in Warsaw, Mr [Anthony] Drexel Biddle and Mr Hillman, 19 July 1939.
N. 124,262: report of Turkish

Ambassador in London, Rüstü Aras, 8 August 1939. [See also *D.B.F.P.*, vol. VI, nos. 207, 225–7.]

76 N. 114,473.

77 N. 115,968 and N. 118,900. [There is no reference to any Anglo-Soviet or Anglo-Turkish discussions on the entry of British warships into the Black Sea in the published official British documents. The discussion of such a proposal would in any case have been distinctly premature at this date.]

78 N. 122,403.

79 N. 122,918.

80 N. 120,341.

81 N. 121,595.

82 N. 124,262.

83 N. 120,003: report of Japanese Ambassador in London, Shigemitsu, dated 10 June 1939.

84 N. 118,035 [report of Turkish Ambassador in Moscow to Foreign Ministry in Ankara, 15 May 1939].

85 N. 118,213 [information of Turkish Foreign Minister to Turkish Ambassador in London, 17 May 1939]. [For the report of the British Ambassador in Ankara on his conversation with M. Saracoglu, see *D.B.F.P.*, vol. V, No. 551.]

86 N. 118,831: information from Turkish Foreign Minister, Saracoglu, for the Turkish Ambassador in Moscow, Apaydin, 22 May 1939, about a despatch from the Turkish Ambassador in London, Rüstü Aras. [For the British record of this conversation, which took place on 19 May, see *D.B.F.P.*, vol. V, no. 615. The German text is an accurate summary.]

87 N. 118,900 [report of Turkish Ambassador in Moscow to Foreign Ministry in Ankara, 24 May 1939].

88 N. 119,328 [report of Japanese Minister in Spain, Yano, 31 May 1939].

89 N. 124,585 [report of Counsellor Adamovic of the Yugoslav Legation in Warsaw, 13 August 1939].

90 N. 119,328 [see Note 88].

91 N. 120,003 [report of Japanese Ambassador in London, 10 June 1939].

92 N. 121,595 [report of Japanese Ambassador in London 1 July 1939].

93 N. 122,403: report of Japanese Minister in Riga, Otaka, 10 July 1939. [For the Latvian Note of 12 June, see D.B.F.P., vol. VI, no. 37.]

94 N. 121,595 [report of Japanese Ambassador in Ankara, Taketomi, 30 June 1939].

95 N. 121,595 [report of Japanese Ambassador in London, Shigemitsu, 30 June 1939].

96 N. 116,207 [despatch from Yugoslav chargé d'affaires in London, Milanovic, 26 April 1939, on an interview with the Soviet chargé d'affaires].

97 [N. 118,213] information from Turkish Foreign Minister Saracoglu for the Turkish Ambassador in London, Rüstü Aras, 17 May 1939. [See Note 71.]

98 N. 121,595 [despatch from Japanese Ambassador in Ankara, 30 June 1939].

99 N. 121,595 [report from Japanese Ambassador in London, 30 June 1939].

100 N. 120,341 [report from Japanese Minister in Stockholm, Kuriyama, 17 June 1939].

101 N. 117,393 [report from Yugoslav chargé d'affaires in London, Milanovic, 9 May 1939].

102 N. 120,003 [report of Japanese Ambassador in London, Shigemitsu, 10 June 1939].

103 N. 118,831: information from Turkish Foreign Minister Saracoglu for the Turkish Ambassador in Moscow, 22 May, on a despatch from the Turkish Ambassador in London Rüstü Aras.

104 N. 119,552: report of Latvian Minister in London Zarine, 6 June 1939.

105 N. 120,003 [report of Japanese Ambassador in London, Shigemitsu, 10 June 1939].

106 N. 121,595 [report of Japanese Ambassador in London, Shigemitsu, 30 June 1939].

107 N. 124,262 [report of Turkish Ambassador in London, Rüstü Aras, 8 August 1939].

108 N. 103,470.

109 N. 95,933 [Andreas Revai, Pester Lloyd, 2 September 1938].

110 [The reference is to the British proposal of 20 March 1939: D.B.F.P., vol. IV, no. 446.]

111 N. 112,958: report of Yugoslav Minister in Warsaw, Vukcevic, 20 March 1939. [For Hudson, see Note 18 to Part I.]

112 [Colonel Beck in fact invited himself to London in February 1939: see D.B.F.P., vol. IV, no. 108.]

113 N. 113,829 [cable from Yugoslav Foreign Minister to Yugoslav Legation in Berlin, 30 March 1939].

114 N. 114,220 [report of Japanese Ambassador in London, Shigemitsu, 31 March 1939. The Yugoslav report of 30 March 1939 does not accord with the evidence of the official British documents.]

115 [*H.C. Deb.*, vol. 345, col. 2415.]

116 N. 114,016 [report of Bulgarian Ambassador in London, 31 March 1939].

117 N. 113,948. [The origins of the British guarantee had little to do with the actions of the Rumanian legation in London. The reports on which action was taken stemmed from Berlin, especially from Mr Ian Colvin, Berlin correspondent of the *News Chronicle*: see *D.B.F.P.*, vol. IV, no. 566, and Ian Colvin, *Vansittart in Office*.]

118 N. 114,472 [see Note 119].

119 N. 114,472 [report from Count Toggenburg, London, 31 March 1939].

120 N. 114,571 [report of Italian Ambassador in Warsaw, Signor Arone, 3 April 1939].

121 N. 113,882 [despatch of Polish Telegraph Agency].

122 N. 113,922 [conversation between Ogilvie-Forbes and Mr G. Ward Price, the British journalist].

123 [That this view *was* held by some members of the British Cabinet is confirmed in J. R. M. Butler, *Grand Strategy*, vol. II, *September 1939–June 1941* (History of the Second World War, United Kingdom Military Series, London, 1957) pp. 59 and 63.]

124 [For Colonel Beck's conversations in London with British Ministers, 4–6 April 1939, and the agreement then reached to conclude a Pact of military assistance between Britain, France and Poland, see *D.B.F.P.*, vol. VI, no. 16.]

125 N. 114,224.

126 N. 114,492 [report of Bulgarian Minister in Paris, Balabanoff, 6 April 1939].

127 N. 114,220.

128 N. 114,491: information of Yugoslav Foreign Minister for the Yugoslav Legation in Berlin, 8 April 1939.

129 N. 115,444 [report of Italian Ambassador in London, 17 April 1939].

130 N. 116,640.

131 N. 117,619. [The *Forschungsamt* was here deliberately misled. Sir Nevile Henderson had requested that instructions to speak in this sense be sent to him in a code the Germans were believed to be able to decipher. Such instructions were sent to him on 11 May, but he did not act on them, and there was no British *démarche* on the 11th. See *D.B.F.P.*, vol V, no. 489, and footnote 2 thereto. The actual British *démarche* was made on 15 May in response to fresh instructions from London: ibid., nos. 513 and 525.]

132 The British mission consisted of Lieutenant-Colonel Clayton, Captain Rowlingson and Mr Davidson (N. 118, 553). On 20 July, General Ironside travelled to Warsaw (Cang, *Manchester Guardian*, 24 July.) [See *D.B.F.P.*, vol, V, nos. 164, 209, 216, 321, 328, 680 and 697; vol. VI, no. 27, footnote 2; and for the visit to Warsaw of General Sir W. Edmund Ironside, the Polish-speaking Inspector-General of the British Armed

Forces, see ibid., nos. 250, 319, 341, 361, 374 and 397; see also *The Ironside Diaries, 1937–1940*.]

133 N. 119,124: Cang, *Manchester Guardian*, 1 June; and N. 119, 231: United Press [report], 2 June. [Mr Strang and Mr Jebb visited Poland in May and early June 1939, returning to London on 9 June: *D.B.F.P.*, vol. V, nos. 659, footnote 2, 721, 735; and vol. VI, no. 16.]

134 [This quotation was originally a footnote. Our translation of the statement has been based on the original English: *H.C. Deb.*, vol. 349, vol. 1788.]

135 N. 122,023 [report from Czech journalist Eisinger in London].

136 N. 121,402.

137 N. 124,274 [conversation between U.S. Ambassador in Warsaw, Mr Anthony Drexel Biddle, and the Hearst newpaper representative in London, 2 August 1939].

138 N. 122,023. [See Note 135. The official British documents do not provide any confirmation of Mr Eisinger's suspicions.]

139 N. 125,763.

140 N. 125,629 [report of the Yugoslav Minister in Warsaw, to Yugoslav Foreign Minister in Belgrade, 23 August 1939. The British-Polish communication referred to a Cabinet statement in this sense published on the evening of 22 August 1939: see *D.B.F.P.*, vol. VII, no. 140, and footnote 3.)

Part III

1 [In his speech in the House of Commons on the Naval Estimates, Mr Duff Cooper had referred to Hitler as 'that thrice-perjured traitor and breaker of oaths'. *H.C. Deb.*, vol. 345, cols. 691–9.]

2 Count Toggenburg of the Munich *N[eueste] N[achrichten]* reported that Stanhope had been 'blind drunk' [*stockbesoffen*], which was characteristic of a man in his position.

3 [See *D.B.F.P.*, vol. V, no. 289; *D.G.F.P.*, vol. VI, no. 272.]

4 Cf. *The Times*, 26 April 1939: 'Letting Germany Know'.

5 [See *H.C. Deb.*, vol. 346, col. 790.]

6 N. 116,236 [despatch by Coulondre, 26 April. For Chamberlain's announcement, see *H.C. Deb.*, vol. 346, cols. 1150–4.]

7 N. 115,829. [No record of this communication appears in the published series of official British documents.]

8 N. 116,086. [No record of these conversations appears in the published series of official British documents.]

9 N. 116,237 [report by Milanovic, 26 April].

10 As is well known, a German Memorandum was also handed to the Polish Government on the same day, containing a declaration that, by accepting the commitments from England, Poland had arbitrarily and unilaterally abrogated the German-Polish Treaty of 26 January 1934. [For the German Memorandum of 27 April denouncing the Anglo-German Naval Agreements see *D.B.F.P.*, vol. V, no. 307; *D.G.F.P.*, vol. VI, no. 277. This Memorandum, in fact, only denounced Part III of the Anglo-German Naval Agreement of 1937, here erroneously described as a declaration.]

11 [See note 131 to Part II above]. N. 117,619.

12 [For the British Memorandum of 27 June, see *D.B.F.P.*, vol. VI, no. 136; *D.G.F.P.*, vol. VI, no. 571.]

13 RW. 228 [a radio monitoring report].

14 N. 115,960. [The original text gives the date as 15 April, which is improbable, as Henderson was still in London at that time. Comparison of other serial numbers suggests that the date should read 25 April: i.e. N. 115,959 was dated 24 April. See also *D.B.F.P.*, vol. VI, no. 61.]

15 N. 122,405. [Telephone] conversation with Mrs Abbott, 14 July 1939. [Mrs Abbott was the wife of the Secretary of the American Legation in Belgrade, whom Sir Nevile Henderson had befriended when he was British Minister there, and who later became American Consul at Hamburg. See Henderson, p. 235. The 'King-Hall letters' were the *Newsletters* of which the British M.P. and journalist Commander Stephen King-Hall distributed five numbers in Germany during the summer of 1939. See *D.B.F.P.*, vol. VI, nos. 337, 395; ibid., Appendix II, no. (iv); *D.G.F.P.*, vol. VI, no. 672; *H.C. Deb.*, vol. 350, col. 901; and Stephen King-Hall, *Total Victory* (London, 1941), pp. 208–11, 283–304.]

16 N. 121,595 [report by Shigemitsu, 1 July 1939. The date was left blank in the original text.]

Part IV

1 [See *D.B.F.P.*, vol. VII, no. 145.]

2 N. 125,365 [telephone conversation of Henderson late on 22 August 1939].

3 N. 125,361 [telephone conversation between Holman and Foreign Office London, 23 August 1939. There is no record of this conversation in the published series of official British documents, but see Berlin telegram no. 442 of 23 August 1939, which was telephoned in cipher to London: *D.B.F.P.*, vol. VII, no. 167.]

4 [For the British record of this conversation, see *D.B.F.P.*, vol. VII, nos. 178, 200 and 248; for the German version see *D.G.F.P.*, vol. VII, no. 200.]

5 N. 125,413 [telephone conversation between Henderson in Salzburg and the British Embassy in Berlin, 23 August. Henderson's report was telephoned onward, *en clair,* from the British Embassy in Berlin to London on the afternoon of 23 August, with minor variations from Henderson's text; see *D.B.F.P.*, vol. VII, no. 178.]

6 N. 125,482 and N. 125,620 [report by Davignon to Brussels, 23 August. This report does not figure in the published series of official Belgian documents.]

7 N. 125,765 [despatch by Attolico to Foreign Ministry in Rome, 24 August. For the full text of this despatch see *D.D.I.*, vol. XIII, no. 214, where its time is given as 11.15 p.m.]

8 N. 125,768 [Henderson's telegram to the Foreign Office, 25 August 1939. For Henderson's reports on this conversation with Hitler, which were made by telegram in the first instance, see *D.B.F.P.*, vol. VII, nos. 283, 284, 288 and 310, the first of which contained the text of Hitler's 'offer': all these telegrams were communicated to London by telephone, but in cipher.]

9 N. 125,767 [telephone conversation between Henderson and Coulondre on the evening of 25 August. For Coulondre's report on his conversation with the British Ambassador, see *French Yellow Book*, No. 245; Robert Coulondre, *De Staline à Hitler, Souvenirs de deux ambassades, 1936–1939* (Paris, 1950) p. 239.]

10 N. 125,775.

11 N. 126,107 (despatch of Turkish chargé d'affaires in London to Ankara].

12 N. 126,513 [despatch of Japanese Ambassador in London to Tokyo].

13 N. 126,514 [despatch of Yugoslav Minister in London to Belgrade].

14 N. 126,051 and N. 125,946.

15 N. 126,247 [For Henderson's reports on this visit to Hitler on 28 August, see *D.B.F.P.*, vol. VII, nos. 450, 455 and 472; for the German version see *D.G.F.P.*, vol. VII, no. 384].

16 N. 126,244 [telephone conversation between Henderson and Coulondre, 9.50 p.m., 28 August. For Coulondre's version of his interview with Henderson at 10 p.m. that evening, before Henderson's visit to the Führer, see Coulondre, pp. 295–6.]

17 N. 126,262.

18 N. 126,372 [Italian Ambassador's despatch telephoned to Rome. For the text of this, see *D.D.I.*, vol. XIII, no. 399].

19 N. 126,269 [despatch of Yugoslav Minister in Berlin to Belgrade (?) For the full text of Chamberlain's re-

ply to Hitler, see *D.B.F.P.*, vol. VII, no. 426].

20 N. 126,409 [despatch of French Ambassador Coulondre telephoned to Paris on 29 August: for full text of this report see *French Yellow Book*, no. 287].

21 N. 126,274 [Foreign Office instruction to British Embassy in Berlin. No record of this instruction appears in the published series of official British documents.]

22 N. 126,294.

23 N. 126,260.

24 N. 126,414 and N. 126,433. [For Henderson's report on this, his second interview with Hitler, and the text of the German note of 28 August, see *D.B.F.P.*, vol. VII, nos. 490, 498, 502 and 508; for Coulondre's report to Paris, on Henderson's information on this interview with Hitler, see *French Yellow Book*, no. 291. Both these reports, British and French, were communicated to their respective Foreign Offices by telephone, but Henderson's (at least) was in cipher. See also *D.G.F.P.*, vol. VII, no. 421].

25 [This communication does not appear in the published series of official British documents.]

26 N. 126,432 [telephone call from British Embassy in Berlin to Foreign Office, London, 30 August. This is presumably the communication published in *D.B.F.P.*, vol. VII, no. 502, and timed as having been received by telephone in London at 12.30 a.m., 30 August. The telegram was communicated *en clair*.]

27 N. 126,452 [presumably a reference to London telegram no. 285 of 30 August, published in *D.B.F.P.*, vol. VII, no. 504; this telegram was sent by telephone but in cipher.]

28 N. 126,487.

29 [This presumption by the *Forschungsamt* was incorrect. Henderson had already seen Josef Lipski, the Polish Ambassador in Berlin, very late on the night of 29/30 August (see *D.B.F.P.*, vol. VII, no. 510); from Attolico's reports (*D.D.I.*, vol. XIII, Nos. 437 and 445), that of Coulondre (*French Yellow Book*, no. 300) and that of Signor Orsenigo, the Papal Nuncio (*D.B.F.P.*, vol. VII, no. 523 and *Actes et documents du Saint Siege relatifs a la seconde querre mondiale, vol. I: La Saint Siege et la guerre en Europe, Mars 1939–1940*, no. 155) these visits would appear to have been purely informative. See also *D.B.F.P.*, vol. VII, no. 516, footnote 2, and no. 522. For Henderson's record of his telephone conversation with Ernst von Weizsäcker, State Secretary in the German Foreign Ministry, at 11 a.m. on 30 August, see ibid., no. 520.]

30 N. 126,588 [communication from Foreign Office, London to British Embassy, Berlin, on 30 August. No record of this appears in the published series of official British documents. For the 'long' telegram see *D.B.F.P.*, vol. VII, no. 543; two related short telegrams are ibid., nos. 534 and 548. They are timed between 5.40 and 9.05 p.m., 30 August.]

31 N. 126,472.

32 N. 126,591.

33 N. 126,609.

34 N. 126,610. [Henderson in fact saw von Ribbentrop at mid-night on 30 August, *D.B.F.P.*, vol. VII, no. 548 footnotes 5, nos. 570 and 571;

Henderson, p. 269; *D.G.F.P.*, vol. VII, no. 461.]

35 N. 127,119. [The German text reproduces almost the exact words of Berlin telegram No. 544, of 2 September, telephoned en clair to London: *D.B.F.P.*, vol. VII, no. 715. The German text talks of *Vermittlungsvorschläge* (mediation proposals) where the British text just states 'proposals'.]

36 [Henderson had in fact seen Lipski a little earlier: 'I nevertheless saw the Polish Ambassador at 2 a.m. . . .' (Henderson, p. 273). His report on this is timed at 5.15 a.m., 31 August (*D.B.F.P.*, vol. VII, no. 575.) He did not reach Lipski again until after 9 a.m. His renewed efforts to get in touch with Lipski were the result of information given to him by Signor Attolico and by the former German Ambassador in Rome, Ulrich von Hassell, both instigated by Ernst von Weizsäcker: see *D.B.F.P.*, vol. VII, nos. 578, 579 and 628; *D.D.I.*, vol. XIII, no. 483; and *The von Hassell Diaries* (London, 1948) entry of 31 August 1939, (p. 69). It should be noted that all the British telegrams listed here were sent to London in cipher.

37 N. 126,644. [There is no published record of such a telephone communication from Henderson to Cadogan at 8.45 a.m. There is a somewhat similarly worded telegram to Lord Halifax, received by telephone at 9.15 a.m., but this communication, which was sent to London en clair, does not contain the very significant addition about "bluffing": *D.B.F.P.*, vol. VII, no. 577. In his telegram of 10.30 a.m., 31 August 1939 (ibid., no. 579

Henderson stated specifically that he did not believe the Germans were bluffing, and this seems to contradict this reported 'addition'.]

38 [For a Foreign Office minute on this conversation with Henderson, see *D.B.F.P.*, vol. VII, no. 578; see also *D.G.F.P.*, vol. VII, no. 466.]

39 N. 126,648 [*D.B.F.P.*, vol. VII, no. 575.]

40 [For Coulondre's report of this conversation, see *French Yellow Book*, no. 315; Coulondre, pp. 300–1.]

41 N. 126,682. [This telegram, which is reproduced almost exactly in the German record, was telephoned *en clair* to London at 11.35 a.m. on 31 August: see *D.B.F.P.*, vol. VII, no. 582. Words printed here in square brackets figure in the German, but not in the published British text.]

42 N. 126,815 [telephone conversation between Henderson and Coulondre, 31 August. Neither this nor the subsequent conversation re-recorded as having taken place between Henderson and Coulondre appears in the published series of official British documents.]

43 N. 126,835 [see Note 42].

44 N. 126,828 [telephone conversation between Ogilvie-Forbes and Orsenigo, the Papal Nuncio: no record of this conversation appears in the published series of official British or Italian documents].

45 N. 126,843 [telephone conversation between Holman and Ogilvie-Forbes, 1 September: the reference is presumably to the document printed in *D.B.F.P.*, vol. VII, no. 620, which was sent to Berlin as a cipher telegram].

46 N. 126,862 [telegram from Henderson to Foreign Office, 1 September: the *Forschungsamt* is apparently referring to Henderson's two consecutive telegrams telephoned in cipher to the Foreign Office and received at 10.45 and 10.50 a.m., 1 September; *D.B.F.P.*, vol. VII, nos. 644 and 645].

47 [The reference would appear to be to *D.B.F.P.*, vol. VII, no. 631, which was sent in cipher by telephone at 12.30 a.m. on 1 September.]

48 N. 126,876 [telephone conversation between Henderson and Coulondre, 1 September: no record of this conversation appears either in the published series of official British documents or in the *French Yellow Book*.]

49 N. 127,005 [telegram from Foreign Office to British Embassy in Berlin, 1 September: see *D.B.F.P.*, vol. VII, no. 669, communicated to Berlin by telephone *en clair*.]

50 N. 127,018 [telephone conversation between Harrison and Stoker, 1 September: no record of this conversation appears in the published series of official British documents.]

51 N. 127,034 [telegrams from Henderson to the Foreign Office, 1 September: see *D.B.F.P.*, vol. VII, nos. 682 and 684; *D.G.F.P.*, vol. VII, nos. 513 and 523. These were sent by telephone to London, *en clair*.

52 N. 127,230 [telegram from Foreign Office to British Embassy in Berlin. See *D.B.F.P.*, vol. VII, no. 732; and *H.C. Deb.*, vol. 351, cols. 126–133.]

53 [See *D.B.F.P.*, vol. VII, no. 735.]

54 N. 127,241 [telephone conversa-

tion between Henderson and Coulondre, 2 September: no record of this conversation appears in either the official British documents or the *French Yellow Book*.]

55 N. 127,240 [telegram from Foreign Office to British Embassy in Berlin: see *D.B.F.P.*, vol. VII, no. 752].

56 N. 127,253 [telephone conversation between Ogilvie-Forbes and unidentified person, 3 September].

57 N. 127,262 [see *D.B.F.P.*, vol. VII, nos. 760, 756 and 757; and *D.G.F.P.*, vol. VII, no. 560].

58 N. 127,294 [telephone conversation between Henderson and Coulondre, 3 September: see also *D.B.F.P.*, vol. VII, no. 763].

59 N. 127,344 [telephone conversation between Henderson and Coulondre, 3 September: see Coulondre, p. 314; *D.G.F.P.*, vol. VII, nos. 561 and 563; and Cmd. 6115 (1939): *Final Report by the Rt. Hon. Sir Nevile Henderson.*]

60 N. 127,322 [report by Holman to Foreign Office, 3 September: see *D.B.F.P.*, vol. VII, nos. 763 and 766; and *D.G.F.P.*, vol. VII, no. 561].

Index